Felt Board Story Times

Roxane Chadwick

Alleyside Press
Fort Atkinson, Wisconsin

Published by Alleyside Press, an imprint of Highsmith Press LLC
Highsmith Press
W5527 Highway 106
P.O. Box 800
Fort Atkinson, Wisconsin 53538-0800
1-800-558-2110

The paper used in this publication meets the minimum requirements of
American National Standard for Information Science — Permanence of
Paper for Printed Library Material. ANSI/NISO Z39.48-1992.

Library of Congress Cataloging in Publication
Chadwick, Roxane.
        Felt board story times / Roxane Chadwick.
            p.   cm.
        Includes bibliographical references (p.).
        ISBN 0-917846-82-6 (softcover)
        1. Flannel boards. 2. Storytelling. 3. Creative activities
    and seat work.   I. Title.
    LB1043.62.C53   1997
    371.3'35–dc20   96-43671

To my mother, Virginia Robbins,
for her understanding, patience, encouragement, and love.

Contents

1. Preparing a Story Time — 9

How to Use this Book — 9

Making a Felt Board and Stand — 11

2. To The Farm — 17

Story: "X. Y. Zeeman at the Farm" — 17

An alien visits a farm.

Additional Activities and Resources — 21

3. Make Believe — 25

Story: "Li Chen's Perfect Place" — 25

A Chinese girl gets lost in her imagination then uses it to find her way home.

Additional Activities and Resources — 31

4. Many Cultures Make Our World — 35

Story: "Empty Shadow" — 35

Folktale from the Cook Islands about why a mountain has a flat top.

Additional Activities and Resources — 42

5. Gifts — 47

Story: "Teddy Bear" — 47

When Maria receives a teddy bear, her mother tells her how Theodore Roosevelt's nickname, Teddy, became the name for stuffed bear cubs.

Additional Activities and Resources — 53

6. Winter Wonderland — 57

Story: "The Groto Lunkers are Coming" — 57

A Modern tale set in Alaska about imaginary beasts and the power of storytelling.

Additional Activities and Resources — 63

7.   Animals We Love   **67**

Story: "Moonlight Mice: A Tale of Love"   67

Two mice, one from the Living Room and
one from the Kitchen meet and fall in love
in the forbidden Hall.

Additional Activities and Resources   73

8.   Color Gallery   **77**

Story: "Picture for Abuelita"   77

A young Puerto Rican girl wants to paint
a perfect picture for her visiting Grandma.

Additional Activities and Resources   82

9.   It's A Wonderful World   **87**

Story: "Bend in the Stream"   87

A boy of few words gets his community to
clean up a stream in the neighborhood.

Additional Activities and Resources   92

10. Celebrate Me   **97**

Story: "Just Plain Horace"   97

A cat wants to be a super cat, then realizes
he is happier being himself.

Additional Activities and Resources   103

11. Families   **107**

Story: "Watch Out for Giant Toes!"   107

A father tells his sick son about a family of
mole crabs.

Additional Activities and Resources   113

1. Preparing a Story Time

Storytelling with Felt Characters for Young childrren

Telling stories to children is both fun and rewarding. I am reminded why I love to tell stories when I hear a child sigh with satisfaction as Li Chen finds her way home in the story "Li Chen's Perfect Place." Or if I am telling the story "X. Y. Zeeman at the Farm" in which the alien is getting the animals' voices mixed up, I am delighted when the children giggle. All you need for a gratifying story time is a few children, these stories, and careful preparation.

Children from ages three to eight love stories. Since they want to know what is happening, they listen intently. Therefore, they learn new words, hear the cadences of our language, and develop a sense of story structure. If stories are orally exciting, children focus on the words, especially those that repeat, rhyme, or are onomatopoeic. They relish the times when they can participate by repeating a phrase. In a time when visual sensations such as television, video, and computer images are so prevalent, the active listening required for storytelling is an important activity.

Storytelling creates a strong bond between the teller and the listeners. By telling a story, an adult can develop a special relationship with many children at once, for each listener feels the story is just for him or her. Since storytelling is a group activity, children develop social skills. They learn to respect each other when they share vicarious experiences together, a visit to a fantasy land, a silly tale, or a bout with a monster. The most important thing they discover from story times is that learning is fun.

Bright visual props such as felt characters help children focus their attention on the stories. Children who learn visually are drawn by the felt pieces and use them as a jumping off point for their imaginations. While the listeners see a character, they have to visualize his motions and reactions with the help of the storyteller's words. They listen intently so they can see the story.

How to Use This Book

Each chapter is built around a theme such as farms or make believe. The original felt story in each chapter uses this theme in a way that will delight children. The themes do not have to be used during a specific month, although some work better in an appropriate season. Winter Wonderland would be best in winter; and the story about mole crabs is suited for warm weather.

You will notice numbers imbedded in each of the felt stories. After each story there is a section explaining how to move the felt characters. The imbedded numbers are reference points for an action or a movement of a felt piece. You may wish to ignore the numbers in your early readings.

The rest of each chapter supplements the story. While the felt story will be new to all the children, the activities and resources will be a mix of familiar and new. A second story, song, or activity provides an informal, often participatory way to reuse the same felt pieces. A supplementary list of resources for the theme is next. These include age appropriate activities, poems, nursery rhymes, books, music, and a few videos. You may select from these to make a story time, lesson day, or weekly theme.

Using Poetry

When reciting a poem, photocopy it, for exact wording is necessary. Tape it to the back of the book since the poems listed have good illustrations. Before reciting the poem to the children, read it aloud until you are familiar with it.

Traditional nursery rhymes form an important part of the basic literary knowledge for young children in our culture. I have found that many children do not know Mother Goose rhymes, especially those who recently have immigrated to our country or whose parents do not share the American cultural background. Children should become familiar with them so they share this common literary base. Use or omit these rhymes depending on the children you teach.

Using Picture Books

Picture books are easy to share with children. A few children can gather around your lap. With a larger group, they need to sit in front of you. Hold the book open for them to see. The better you know the story, the steadier you can hold the book. When you peek at the text, the movement often interrupts the children's view of the pictures and breaks their concentration. I have chosen titles with bright illustration, multicultural representation, and good stories. A few special books are longer. Try to use only one of these at a time.

Music/Video Resources

The music resources I have listed include a cassette or CD source for songs to be listened to, the written music and words for singing, or both. For use in week-long themes, I have listed a few videos for variety.

Structuring Story Sessions or Circle Times

When it's time for a story session or circle time, I shake a tambourine that makes an exciting sound and, like the Pied Piper, I lead the children into the story room. Find some signal for calling the children that works for you. My small, story room has large paintings of favorite storybook characters on the walls, Frog and Toad, one of the Wild Things, Titch, Spot, and Curious George. It is an ideal place for stories because it is quiet, has a soft rug for sitting on, and is away from distractions. Find a regular, quiet place that is free from interruptions for your stories. After everyone is settled, the children and I stand and sing our opening song to the tune of "London Bridge":

> Story time has just begun.
> Clap, clap, clap, just begun.
> Story time has just begun.
> Let's have fun.

In this little ritual the children and I clap during lines two and four. The song reminds them it is time to listen and gives them a moment to participate together before sitting for the stories.

Keep story sessions short and fun, gaining length as the children's attention spans increase. For beginners, 30 minutes or less is plenty. Before long, they will probably work their way up to 40 minutes. Shorter, more frequent story sessions are more rewarding for both listener and teller.

A variety of storytelling forms and lengths, interspersed with stretches, poems, and songs will keep even the most active child interested. Just be sure to quit BEFORE they have had enough and while they are still eager to continue. I end story time with a song similar to our beginning song. Again to the tune of "London Bridge," we clap and sing:

Story time is all done.
Clap, clap, clap. It's all done.
Story time is all done.
We had fun.

Art and Other Activities

Separate story time or listening time from craft and play time. Art activities, games, and discussions are a less structured activity where children have more opportunity to express their individualism. These activities also play an important part in children's development. I have suggested some simple crafts and activities that relate to the themes of the stories, but if the children's creativity propels them in opposite directions, this is the time to let them go their own way.

Learning the Stories

After you have planned your story session by choosing a variety of the stories, activities, and resources from this book, the next step is to learn and practice telling the stories. Think of the telling as a gift from you to the children. It is not a performance.

Since these stories are short and simple, they are easy to learn. Reading them aloud several times should imprint them in your mind. Think about the logical order of events. Use the felt characters to jog your memory. After you have learned the story, try telling it at least twice aloud to be sure there are no rough edges. Smooth them out by referring to the text. A friend of mine likes to make a tape recording of herself telling the story, and she listens to it while driving to work. Another practices in front of a mirror. Choose whatever method is fun for you and fits into your schedule.

These stories are plot-driven and precise wording is not necessary. Sometimes I memorize the beginning and ending phrases so I can be free to

watch the excitement or contentment in the children's faces. When you are ready to tell the stories, put the text nearby, and watch those shy eyes glitter with anticipation.

Preparing the Felt Characters

The felt characters are right here for you to use. Just photocopy them onto white or colored paper, filling in other colors with markers or dry watercolors. I must warn you that some markers, usually the expensive, artist's ones, smear the lines from some types of photocopiers, so test your markers first. Cutting has been simplified by smoothing the felt character's outlines so you can save time with this procedure. Next, glue the cutout characters to felt with either a glue stick or rubber cement. Press the finished characters in books while drying to keep them flat. I sandwich them between clean white sheets of paper to prevent the marker colors or the glue from getting on the book's pages. Then, trim around the felt, and they are ready to use.

Making a Felt Board and Stand

Making a Felt Board

You can purchase a felt board and stand or you can easily make one. Cover a lightweight foam board, 24"x36", with a large piece of felt. Neutral shades of blues and grays show off colorful characters best, but any color works. Be sure to cut the felt at least 4" wider and taller than the board. Do not glue the felt to the board because glue inhibits the ability of the felt characters to stick to the felt board. Fold the extra 2" of felt onto the back of the board. Tape the felt's edges to the back of the board with cloth tape.

You will need to glue Velcro strips that are ¾" wide to the back to attach the board to the homemade stand. I use the softer half of the Velcro on the board and the tougher strips on the stand.

Position three strips, 11" long, parallel to the bottom of the board at 4", 8", and 12" from the bottom. Center the strips along the longer side of the board. Repeat this procedure using the shorter side of the board. Finally, tape the ends of the Velcro strips to make them stay put longer. The six Velcro strips will enable the board to stand with either the longer or shorter side at the bottom. *(See figure 1.)*

Making a felt Board Stand

Make a stand from a cardboard box that is about 13"x12"x16". Any similar size will work well. The smallest end of the box will be the front of the stand, the part that will attach to the felt board. Write "front" on it. The longer sides of the box will form the wings. Write "wings" on the two longer sides near the edge that attaches to the front. These three sections remain attached and form the main part of the stand.

Cut off the fourth side and the bottom of the box. I prefer using a knife for cutting cardboard. Remove all extra flaps, so you have three sides attached at two corners. Shorten each wing to 12" long.

Measure 1" up from the bottom corner of a wing. From this point, draw a straight line to the bottom of the fold that connects the wing to the front. Repeat on the other side. *(See figure 2.)* Cut along these lines. This new cut will become the bottom of the wings and will let the felt board tilt backward for easier use.

Next, measure 2½" down from the top edge along the outer edge of the wing. Cut a slit about 1½" deep and parallel to the top. I find scissors more practical than a knife for this cut. Repeat this procedure for the other wing. *(See figure 2.)*

Glue three, 11", Velcro strips vertically on the front of the stand. Put one down the center and one on each side of the center strip, about 4" away. Again, reinforce the strips by taping the ends.

Cut a separate strip of cardboard about 18" long and 3" to 4" wide. This piece will be the brace. Along one long edge of the brace, mark two points that are 2" from the short ends. At each point cut a 1½" slit. The brace is now complete. *(See figure 3.)*

When you are ready to use the stand, insert the slits in the brace into the slits in the wings. *(See figure 4.)* Press the Velcro pieces of the board into those of the stand. The board is now ready for stories. When you're finished telling your stories, you can disassemble the stand and board for convenient storage in an artist's portfolio.

Figure 1: Back of Felt Board (2'x 3')

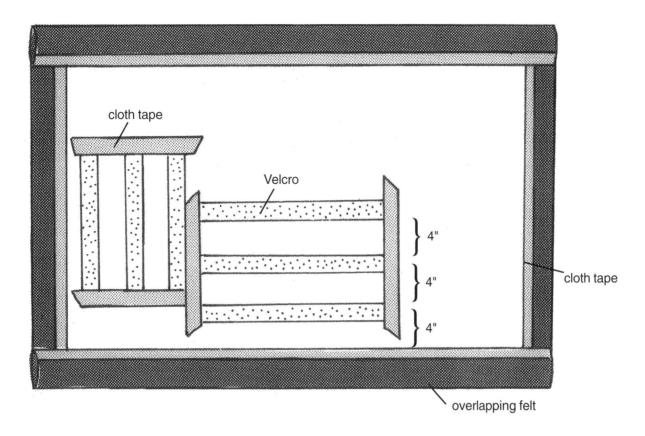

cloth tape

Velcro

4"

4"

4"

cloth tape

overlapping felt

Figure 2: Stand for Board

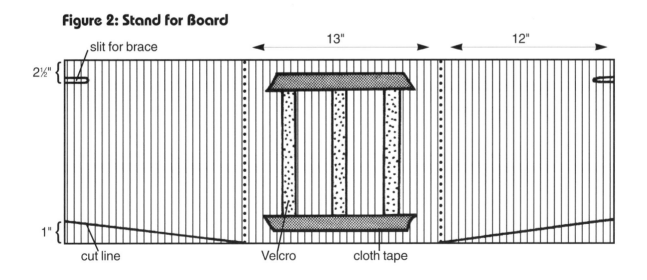

slit for brace

2½"

13"

12"

1"

cut line

Velcro

cloth tape

Figure 3: Brace

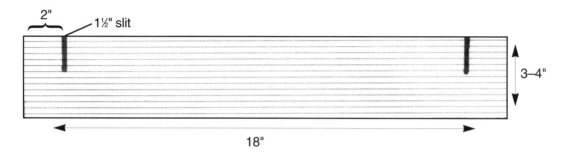

2"

1½" slit

3–4"

18"

Figure 4: Felt Board with Stand Attached

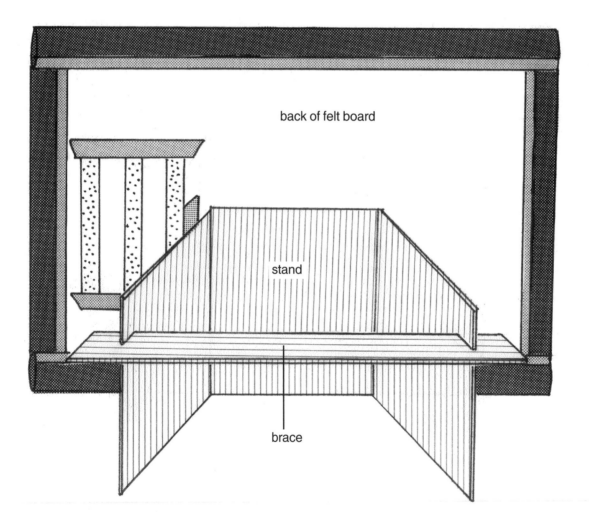

back of felt board

stand

brace

2. To the Farm

Introduction

Children will love visiting an imaginary farm with you. If you use a familiar theme and simple stories for your beginning program, the children can concentrate on learning the routine and developing listening skills. New concepts will be easier to learn later when they have learned the pattern of story times and feel at ease with the storyteller.

The story, "X. Y. Zeeman at the Farm," is a humorous, participation story. Children giggle at the incongruity of a "moo" coming from a horse, and X. Y. Zeeman's lack of knowledge about animal sounds delights children. They feel proud that they know more about farm animals and their sounds than the know-it-all, alien visitor.

Before beginning the story, spend a few minutes making the shy ones in your group feel at ease. A technique that often works is to get down on the floor with them and ask them questions about themselves. Be sure to tell them ahead of time that you might need a little help with the story. Then, when you ask them to respond, they will be eager to join in.

Felt Board Story

X. Y. Zeeman at the Farm

One clear, crisp day X. Y. Zeeman, ❶ an alien from outer space, visited Farmer Brown ❷ in Apple Valley, Maryland. ❸ X. Y. Zeeman wanted to visit the farm and see the animals that lived in the barn. He thought he would know everything about them. As they neared the barn, the know-it-all alien could hardly keep his ears from flapping with excitement. From inside the barn came a loud, "Moo. Moo."

Farmer Brown started to say, "That is my … ," but the alien interrupted.

"Do not tell me." His big ears wiggled. "Let me guess, for I know almost everything. Is that a horse?" ❹

Farmer Brown said, "No, that is not a horse." He looked at the grass, the rusty hinges of the barn door, and the clouds so he would not stare at the alien's wiggling ears.

"Is it a dog?" guessed X. Y. Zeeman.

"No," said Farmer Brown. "It is a cow." ❺ The jolly farmer opened the barn door that creaked and shimmied as it swung wide. "Let's look inside at my cow," ❻ he said. He knew a lot about cows but very little about spacemen.

"Moo," said the cow.

"A cow says, 'Moo,'" said X. Y. Zeeman. "Now, I know everything." He was touching the cow's back and saying, "Twark, twark," when another sound came from nearby.

"Neigh."

"Do not tell me," said the alien, his big ears rippling like waves. "Is that a pig?" ❼

The farmer laughed and felt he was growing smarter by the minute. "No, a pig does not say 'Neigh.'"

"Is it a hen?" X. Y. Zeeman asked. His ears were flapping so fast, Farmer Brown thought he might fly away.

"No," said Farmer Brown. "It is a ❽ horse. He stepped over to the next stall to introduce his friend to the horse. ❾

"Neigh," whinnied the horse.

"A horse goes 'neigh,'" said X. Y. Zeeman. "Now, I know everything." He had touched the soft nose of the horse and was saying, "Twark, twark," when another strange sound came from nearby.

"Oink, oink."

"Do you want to guess?" Farmer Brown asked his visitor from outer space. He liked this curious fellow and was enjoying the guessing game.

"Oh, yes," he answered and wiggled his whole body in excitement. "Does a dog say, 'Oink?'" ❿

"No, my friend, a dog does not say 'oink,'" said Farmer Brown.

"Is it a goat?"

"No, it is a ⓫ pig. Come over here and meet my pig." ⓬

When the alien peered in a dark corner, he saw a fat, pink pig, who greeted him with an oink.

"And an oink to you too," said X. Y. Zeeman. "Now, I must know everything!" He had just leaned over to pat the pig when a high-pitched sound came from outside the barn.

"Yoo-hoo! Yoo-hoo!"

X. Y. Zeeman's ears began to wiggle. He said, "Twark, twark. Do not tell me," but he looked puzzled. "It is not a cow or a horse or a pig."

"No," said Farmer Brown. "Maybe you had better not guess this one." Into the barn stepped a pretty woman. ⓭ "This is my wife. Mrs. Brown meet X. Y. Zeeman."

"Yoo-hoo to you too," said the visitor.

Mrs. Brown asked, "Have you been learning about our animals? My Bill here knows just about everything there is to know about farm animals."

"Yes, I now know everything too." The spaceman wiggled all over. "I heard a moo that came from a ⓮ cow and a neigh that came from a ⓯ horse and an oink that came from a ⓰ pig. And I heard a yoo-hoo that came from ⓱ you."

"Good for you," said Mrs. Brown patting him on a shoulder. Now you must teach me what they say on your planet."

"Guess," he said. That know-it-all look crossed his face once again.

"Twark, twark?" asked Mrs. Brown.

His eyes grew big and his ears drooped. "You must be the one who knows everything."

"No," said Mrs. Brown. "But just like you, I listen so I can learn. You teach us about your planet, and we'll teach you about ours. Then, we'll all know a lot more." And that's exactly what the three of them did.

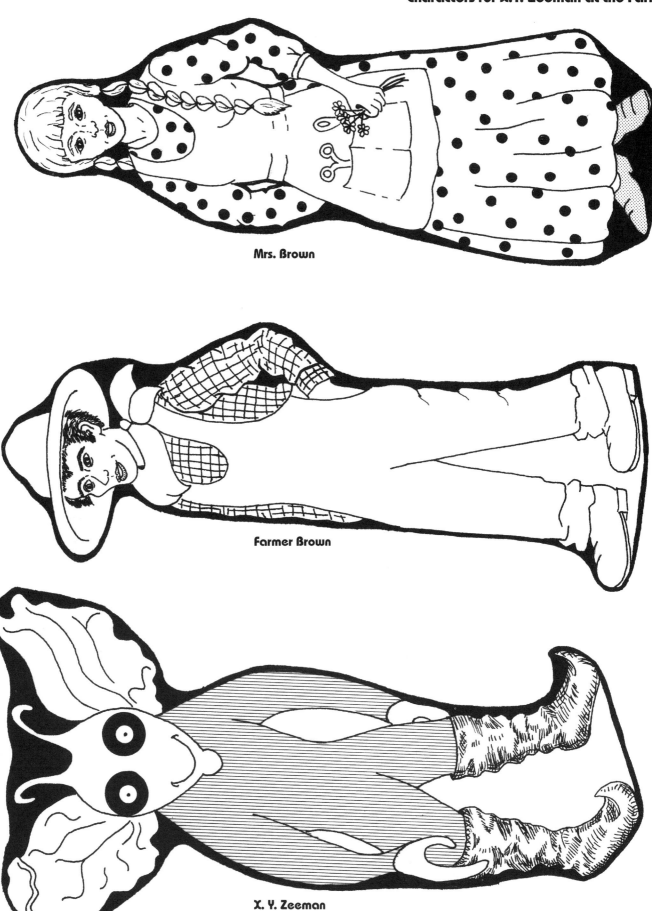

Mrs. Brown

Farmer Brown

X. Y. Zeeman

Characters for X.Y. Zeeman at the Farm

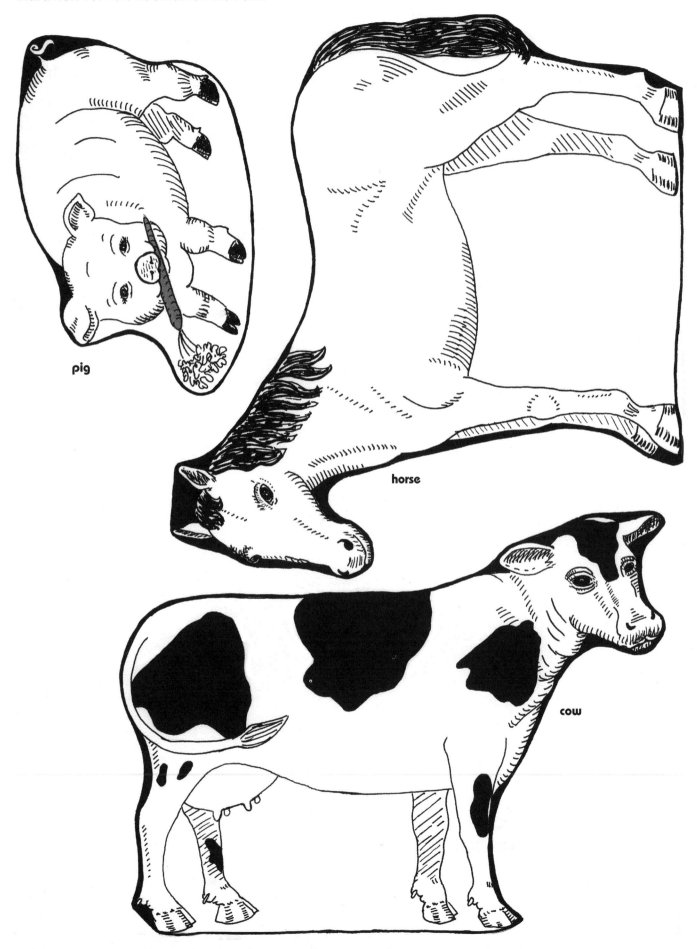

pig

horse

cow

Movements of Felt Characters

"X. Y. Zeeman at the Farm" is the simplest kind of felt story. Each character is placed on the board then left until the story is finished. You will need to practice the movements only once to know when to add a character and how to space the pieces evenly on the felt board.

For this story put the longer side of the felt board horizontally. Right and left directions assume you are facing the board.

❶ Position X. Y. Zeeman near the center of the board.

❷ Add Farmer Brown to the right of him.

❸ Substitute the local state for Maryland if you wish.

❹ Shake your head and urge the children to respond by asking, "Well, is it?" When they say, "No," continue. Even if they do not participate, go on with the story.

❺ Pause to let the children say "cow".

❻ Place the cow on the board to the left of the alien.

❼ Stop telling the story and encourage the children to participate.

❽ Wait for the children to name the animal.

❾ Add the horse to the right of Farmer Brown.

❿ Shake your head to draw the children's response.

⓫ Pause for the children to supply the animal's name.

⓬ Put the pig on the board to the left of the cow.

⓭ Position Mrs. Brown to the right of the horse.

⓮ Let the children fill in the correct animal. Repeat for ⓯ and ⓰.

⓱ Wait to see if the children will name Mrs. Brown.

The story ends with all the felt pieces on the board.

Second Activity Using Characters

"Old MacDonald Had a Farm"

A natural activity to follow this story is to use the felt characters to sing the song, "Old MacDonald Had a Farm." Start with the farmer on the board and add an animal for each verse. When the three animals are finished, try Mrs. Brown and have her say, "Yoo-hoo." Next, sing a verse for X. Y. Zeeman. Of course, he says, "Twark, twark." After using all the felt characters, you can add some silly fun by singing about other things that a farmer might have, like a car, a baby, or an airplane.

A good cassette source for this song is *Wee Sing* by Pamela Beall and Susan Nipp. Los Angeles: Price Stern Sloan, 1981. The music and words can be found in *Tom Glazer's Treasury of Songs for Children*, Garden City, New York: Doubleday, 1964.

Creative Activities

Science Activity: Learn about Apples

Let your young scientists examine apples by using all their senses. Let them feel the outside skin, look at the color, twist the stem, and find the flower end. Cut the apple in half horizontally to reveal the star pattern of the seeds. Let them listen for the crunching sound when it is cut and eaten. Let them touch, smell, and taste the moist white fruit.

Art Activity: Make a Spaceman Puppet

Take a small paper bag and let the children stick various pre-cut shapes on the bag: streamers, stars, circles, doilies. Use paste or glue sticks. Once they have their own spaceman puppet, suggest that the children give it a name, tell about its home, and guess who it thinks says "Moo."

Field Trip: Visit a Farm

A dairy farm, especially at milking time, is fun to visit. After the trip, make butter by putting a half pint of room temperature, whipping cream into a jar about twice the size of the liquid. With the children in a circle, let them roll the jar back and forth until it becomes butter. It takes about 20 minutes of shaking or rolling for butter to be formed. To pass the time, play music and chant this nursery rhyme:

> Come, butter, come,
> Come, butter, come;
> Peter stands at the gate
> Waiting for a butter cake.
> Come, butter, come.

When finished, pour off the remaining buttermilk, spread the butter on salted crackers, and taste. If you choose a glass jar, be sure to take proper precautions. A half pint of cream makes about a half cup of butter.

Resources for Story Time

Poems

"Hickety, Pickety, My Black Hen." From *The Real Mother Goose*, Chicago, Ill.: Rand McNally, 1916.

When repeating this nursery rhyme, cut out the shape of an egg from a stack of thin white paper, nine or ten pages thick. Afterwards count the eggs aloud together to see how many there are. Sometimes there are nine; sometimes, ten.

"My Little Dad Had Five Little Piggies." From *It's Raining Said John Twaining*, translated by N. M. Bodecker. New York: Atheneum, 1973.

A Danish nursery rhyme with a fanciful illustration.

"Fruits" by Opal Palmer Adisa. From *A Caribbean Dozen: Poems From Caribbean Poets*, edited by John Agard and Grace Nichols. Cambridge, Mass.: Candlewick, 1994.

A two-page, color illustration of fruits found at the market. Share a variety of fruits with the children after reading the poem.

Books

Buzz, Buzz, Buzz by Byron Barton. New York:Aladdin, 1995.

Reissue of an old favorite. A bee stings a bull and starts an unusual chain of events.

Great Pig Escape by Eileen Christelow. New York:Clarion, 1994.

Hilarious story about two farmers who decide to add pigs to their farm.

Busy Monday Morning by Janina Domanska. New York:Greenwillow, 1985.

A simple dramatization of a Polish song about a child helping his father with the hay. Music for the song is in the back of the book.

Barnyard Banter by Denise Fleming. New York:Holt, 1994.

Animal sounds abound in this simple, colorful book.

Mary Had a Little Lamb. Rhyme by Sarah Hale. New York: Scholastic, 1990.

Illustrated with photographs by Bruce McMillan. Wonderful pictures of a bespectacled, African-American girl and her lamb to go with the familiar rhyme.

How the Ox Star fell From Heaven by Lily Toy Hong. Morton Grove, Ill.: Whitman, 1991.

This Chinese folktale tells how the Ox Star came to earth and became a beast of burden to help people grow food.

The Day the Goose Got Loose by Reeve Lindbergh. New York: Dial, 1990.

A rhyming story about the havoc caused when the goose gets loose on the farm.

Midnight Farm by Reeve Lindbergh. New York: Dial, 1987.

This short, soothing poem about a farm at midnight is beautifully illustrated by Susan Jeffers.

Lucky Russell by Brad Sneed. New York: Putnam, 1992.

A kitten wants to find an important job on the farm.

This Is the Farmer by Nancy Tafuri. New York: Greenwilow, 1994.

Simple introduction to a farm with large bold illustrations.

Farmer Duck by Martin Waddell. Cambridge, MA: Candlewick, 1991.

When a lazy farmer leaves all the chores to an overworked duck, the animals take matters into their own hands. Sly humor.

Pig In The Pond by Martin Waddell. Cambridge, Mass.: Candlewick, 1992.

On a hot day, a pig watches the geese and ducks in the pond, and finally jumps in. Lively illustrations.

Music

"Cluck, Cluck, Red Hen." Cassette source: *The Corner Grocery Store*, lyrics adapted by Jacquelyn Reinach and sung by Raffi. Willowdale, Ont.: Troubador, 1979.

This song has several verses about farm animals and the products that they give us including "Baa, Baa, Black Sheep."

"Six Little Ducks." Cassette source: *More Singable Songs* by Raffi. Hollywood, Calif.: A & M Records, 1977. Music source: *Raffi Singable Songbook*. New York: Crown, 1980.

I sing this with a duck finger puppet with a feather glued to its tail. Encourage the children to flap their "wings," walk like a duck, and join in at the "quack, quack, quack."

Video

Barnyard Buddies by Harlan and Joyce Meyer. Boardman, Ohio: JTC Inc. 1991.

A visit to a farm with songs, music, and a few preschoolers. Preschool to kindergarten. A bit young for more sophisticated first and second graders. 30 min.

3. Make Believe

Introduction

Pretending comes naturally to children. They love to make believe they are pirates, dogs, mommies, dragons or other real or imaginary beings. This chapter celebrates make believe and is especially useful in October when Halloween traditions allow children to dress up in fanciful costumes.

The story, "Li Chen's Perfect Place," is about a Chinese girl's imaginative journey. When she becomes lost in her fantasy world, she creates a Chinese unicorn or ki-lin (KEE-lin), who gives her a picture-map that shows her the way home.

Before beginning the story explain to the children that some things have more than one name. For example, a bottle of Coke might be called soda by one person and pop by another. People from another country might have a different name for the same object. A hat in Spanish is a sombrero. A Chinese unicorn is called a ki-lin (KEE-lin).

Felt Board Story

Li Chen's Perfect Place

Once there was a faded little house ❶ in China that had wind-bells that sang *tin-ta-ting-ing-ing*. In that house Li Chen lived with her mother and father. Li Chen loved her parents but dreamed of living in a shiny palace surrounded by gardens and beautiful animals.

The wind blew one day and swung the wind-bells, which chimed *tin-ta-ting-ing-ing* calling Li Chen ❷ outside to play. Since she had few toys, she used her amazing imagination for fun. When she thought about something, it almost became real.

Li Chen thought of flowers growing by a gate. She closed her eyes and saw chrysanthemums clustered around a stone gate. When she opened her eyes, ❸ she saw the flowers, smelled them, and walked through the gate into a magical place. ❹

This time she thought of a peacock ❺ in his royal robe of metallic blues, greens, and golds.

He stood still, glistening in the sun as she touched his feathers, soft as silk. ❻

Squeezing her eyes tightly shut, she imagined a river with leaping fish. And then, from the hills flowed a river ❼ as green as jade that rushed over rocks and stopped in a pool by her feet.

Li Chen was happy in her special place until she heard *tin-ta-ting-ing-ing*. She looked for the wind-bells and her faded little house but could not see them. She turned around and looked right and then left but found no way home.

Last night her mother had told her a bedtime story about a Chinese unicorn or ki-lin. This animal had risen from the Yellow River and given the Chinese Emperor Fu Hsi (FOO-shee) a written language for his people. Li Chen wondered if she could use the magic of make believe to find her way home.

Li Chen squeezed her eyes tightly shut and

imagined a ki-lin. ❽ Quickly she opened them wide. Nearby knelt a horselike animal with a single, silver horn sprouting from its forehead. ❾ When Li Chen touched the beautiful horn, she saw a scroll tied on the ki-lin's back.

She took the scroll ❿ and unrolled the paper. She saw a map ⓫ and knew just what to do. ⓬ She would follow the pictures on the map. ⓭

She marched from the ki-lin to the river, ⓮ then to the peacock. From the bird, she ran to the flowered gate ⓯ and through it. ⓰

In the mist she saw the little faded house ⓱ and heard the wind-bells sing *tin-ta-ting-ing-ing* welcoming her home. Li Chen never looked back to see if the flowery gate, the peacock, and the ki-lin were still there.

house

map

scroll

peacock

Characters for Li Chen's Perfect Place

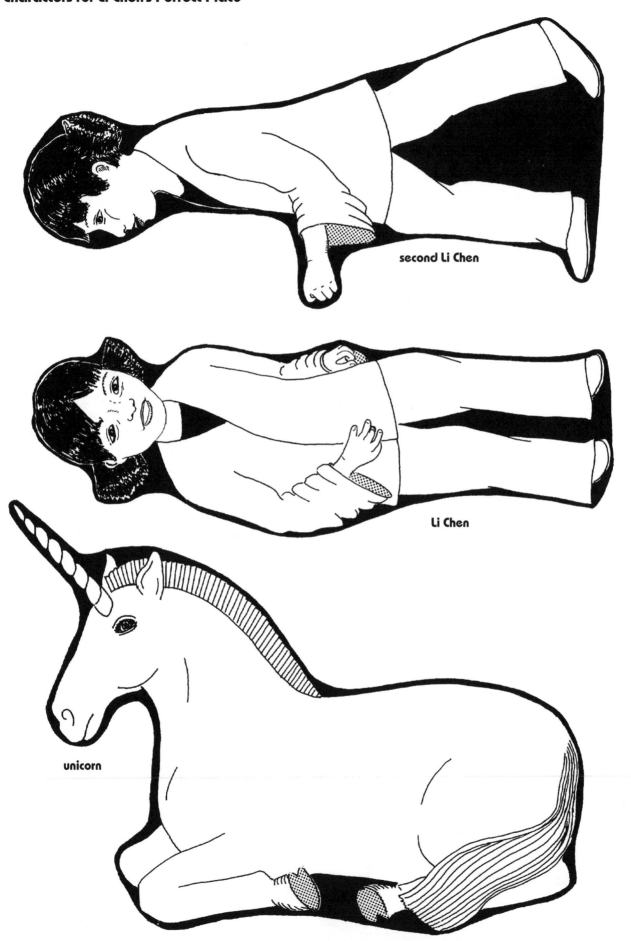

second Li Chen

Li Chen

unicorn

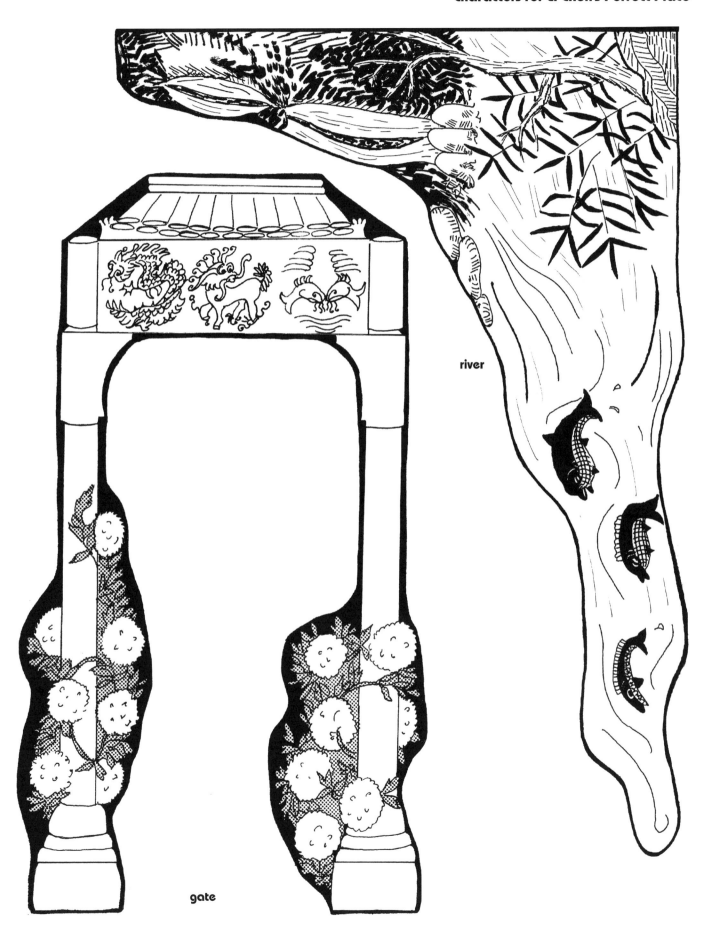

river

gate

Hints for Coloring the Characters

The wind-bells on the house are an important element in the story. Color them a noticeable color like red. The peacock should be metallic blues, greens, and gold. The river is "green as jade." Unicorns are white, and this one's horn is silver. Color both Li Chens the same since this story takes place in one continuous time. Otherwise, use your imagination to color these felt pictures.

Movements of Felt Characters

The movements for this story are of medium complexity. The picture of the house is used twice; therefore, it must be put on the board, removed, and then replaced later. There are two pictures for Li Chen. One is used going into her magical world, and the other is used coming out of that world. Also, both pictures of Li Chen move during the story. Once these complexities are understood, it is easy to position the pictures.

For this story, position your felt board with the longer side horizontal. All left and right directions assume you are facing the front of the board.

❶ Put the picture of the house in the upper left corner.

❷ Place Li Chen, the one facing slightly forward, below the house.

❸ Position the gate to the right of Li Chen.

❹ Walk Li Chen through the gate by moving her in front of the gate until she is on the other side. At this point remove the house. Set the house aside for it will be used again.

You will be positioning the next four large pieces (peacock, river, unicorn, and the second Li Chen) to the right of the gate in a Z pattern. This is a good time to mentally divide this area so the pieces can be spaced easily.

❺ Add the peacock above and to the right of Li Chen.

❻ Move Li Chen to the right of the peacock.

❼ Place the river to the right and slightly below Li Chen.

❽ Put the ki-lin below the peacock and add the scroll on top of his back.

❾ Move Li Chen to the left of the unicorn.

❿ Take the scroll off the board. This piece will not be used again.

⓫ Position the map to the right of the ki-lin, placing it horizontally so it mirrors the figures on the felt board.

⓬ Remove the first Li Chen and place the second Li Chen, the one striding left, to the right of the map.

⓭ Remove the map.

⓮ Put the second Li Chen between the river and the peacock.

⓯ Move the second Li Chen to the right of the gate, and to the left of the gate at **⓰** .

⓱ Add the house in the upper left corner.

As the story ends, the house is in the upper left corner. Below it is the second Li Chen. To the right is the gate, the peacock, the river, and the unicorn.

Second Activity Using Characters

Clever Sisters

Pretend that the two Li Chens are Li Chen and her sister, Mu Tan. Begin to tell the story:

⊱─◈─○─◈─⊰

Once there were two sisters, Li Chen and Mu Tan, who looked very much alike. **(Place the two characters on the felt board.)** They were both pretty. They were both smart. And they both tried to be more clever than each other.

As they wandered together through the willow trees on their journey home, a peacock strutted across their path. **(Add the peacock.)** "That is a big bird," said Li Chen.

"Yes," said Mu Tan. She searched for words more clever than her sister's. "It is a fowl of many colors."

"Yes," said Li Chen. "But it's a gold, green, and blue feathered animal."

"Yes," said Mu Tan. "It's a feather-de-do."

And suddenly the proud peacock strutted away. **(Remove the peacock.)**

Further down the path in an opening, they found a gate. **(Add the gate.)** "That is a flower gate," said Li Chen.

"Yes," said Mu Tan. "But…"

⊱─◈─○─◈─⊰

Continue the story. Have the girls make up different names or ways to describe the gate until you have used a total of four. Then repeat the pattern using the unicorn, river, and map. Ask the children to help make up descriptions or even nonsense words for the object. Accept all names or descriptions. End the story with the following:

⊱─◈─○─◈─⊰

Li Chen and Mu Tan dragged the toes of their shoes slower and slower down the path toward home for they were becoming tired. **(Add the house in the distance.)** "You are my sister," said Li Chen.

"Yes, you are my twin," said Mu Tan.

"Yes," said Li Chen, "and you are my playmate."

"And you are my friend," said Mu Tan. Then the two sisters joined hands, laughed, and ran the rest of the way home.

⊱─◈─○─◈─⊰

Creative Activities

Physical Activity: Walk a Tight Rope

Lay a 2" x 4" inch board on the ground and let the children walk on the 4" side, pretending they are walking on a tight rope above a circus tent. Have them imagine what they are wearing and what tricks they will perform.

Art and Language Activity: Make Leaf Animals

Glue a leaf to a piece of construction paper. Let the children add legs, tails, arms, or wings with crayons or markers. Ask the children to tell about their leaf animal. What noise does it make? What does it like to eat? Where does it live? Encourage and accept all responses no matter how wild or mundane.

Science Activity: Follow a Map to a Treasure

Draw a rough map of your classroom. If you have a safe area and good weather, this activity could be done outside. Mark a trail on the map for the children to follow marking several check points with X's. At each checkpoint put scraps of paper with one letter on it, P for the first checkpoint, R for the second. Continue until the word PRIZE is spelled out. Have the children follow the map like Li Chen followed the unicorn's map. The children could go in small groups or individually. Remind them that they must pick up a letter at each checkpoint. The pile of letters could be under a wastebasket, in a bowl, in a paper bag, or any other accessible but not easily noticed place. Give the children a small prize when they have accumulated all the letters.

Language Activity: Describe a Costume

What might you wear to look like a cat? What would you use for ears? Or a tail? Or whiskers? How would you move? Ask the children these questions for a variety of characters such as a king, a pirate, a rabbit, an alien, an old woman, a mermaid, a fruit salad, and a dragon. Encourage them to see similarities between items, such as an elephant's trunk and a roll of newspaper or a knee-high sock.

Resources for Story Time

Poems

"The Cat and the Fiddle." From *The Real Mother Goose*. Chicago, Ill.: Rand McNally, 1916.

A popular, nonsense nursery rhyme.

"Graceful Elephant." From *Arroz Con LeChe, Popular Songs and Rhymes from Latin America*, translated by Lulu Delacre. New York: Scholastic, 1989.

A Mexican nursery rhyme in English and Spanish. Act out the rhyme by adding one child (an elephant) to balance on the imaginary spider's web in the center of a circle at each verse. Or listen to the American version "One Elephant Went out to Play." Cassette source: *Wee Sing* by Pamela Beall and Susan Nipp. Los Angeles, Calif.: Price Stern Sloan, 1981. Again add a child at each verse. With a large group, count by fives.

Tale of Custard the Dragon by Ogden Nash. Boston: Little, Brown, 1995.

A picture book edition of the humorous poem about a pirate and Belinda with her "relio, trulio, little pet dragon."

Books

Patrick's Dinosaur by Carol Carrick. New York: Tichnor & Fields, 1983.

While visiting the zoo with his brother, Patrick imagines dinosaurs. Great for all dinosaur lovers.

Abuela by Arthur Dorros. New York: Dutton, 1991.

Rosalba, a young Hispanic American, and her grandmother fly on their imaginations over New York City. An energetic story, sprinkled with Spanish words and phrases.

The Wizard Next Door by Peter Glassman. New York:Morrow, 1993.

Only the boy notices the strange magic of the wizard next door. A delight.

Amazing Grace by Mary Hoffman. New York: Dial, 1991.

Grace, an African American girl, loves to act out exciting parts in stories. When her class plans the play *Peter Pan*, Grace proves she can be anything she wants to be.

The Trek by Ann Jonas. New York: Greenwillow, 1985.

On her walk to school, a girl imagines a jungle and desert full of animals. Simple and fun.

Pretend You're a Cat by Jean Marzollo. New York:Dial, 1990.

Wonderful paintings by Jerry Pinkney show children acting like various animals. Children cannot resist joining in.

Tar Beach by Faith Ringgold. New York:Crown, 1991.

Based on the author's quilt painting, this story is about a girl who flies over her Harlem home and claims all she sees.

We're Going on a Bear Hunt, retold by Michael Rosen. New York: Macmillan, 1989.

The traditional chant in a picture book format is fun for a group to act out.

Princess by Susan Roth. New York: Hyperion, 1993.

A little girl insists if she were a princess, her life would be different.

Hurricane by David Wiesner. New York: Clarion, 1990.

When an elm tree falls, two brothers use it as part of their adventures in the jungle, on the seas, out in space.

Chocolate Mud Cake by Harriet Ziefert. New York: Harper, 1988.

Jenny and Molly make a mud cake at Grandma's.

Music

"You Can Fly! You Can Fly! You Can Fly!" From Walt Disney's *Peter Pan.* Compact disk source: *The Music of Disney* Burbank, Calif.: Walt Disney Records, 1992.

Video

Tuesday based on the book by David Wiesner. Hightstown, N.J.: American School Publishers, 1992.

One Tuesday evening in a small town, frogs float through the air while people sleep. 6 min.

4. Many Cultures Make Our World

Introduction

This chapter celebrates the rich diversity that makes up our world and our country. Young children enjoy these simple tales and activities from many cultures. Some stories show how alike all people are while others point out fascinating differences.

The felt board story, "Empty Shadow," is an adaption of a legend from the Cook Islands. The Cook Islands are a group of fifteen Polynesian islands in the Pacific Ocean. The story takes place on Rarotonga (rahr-ah-TOHN-gah), the largest of the islands, and Aitutaki (AH-ee-too-tah-kee), a small island located 140 miles north of Rarotonga.

The second activity with the felt characters, "The Riddling Princess," is based on a motif frequently used in the folklore of many countries. Three suitors compete for the hand of a maiden by solving riddles. The man who correctly answers the most riddles wins the princess's hand.

The resources in this chapter introduce children to Mexico, Russia, China, Vietnam, Africa, Japan, and the Caribbean. There are also stories about Eskimos, Native Americans, African Americans, Korean Americans, and Hispanics.

Felt Board Story

Empty Shadow

Long ago at dawn, the sun spread its golden light in the East. ❶ But the sunbeams did not reach the village of Puaikura, (poo-ah-ee-KOO-rah) ❷ on the west side of the island of Rarotonga (rahr-ah-TOHN-gah) because the shadow ❸ of the great mountain, Maru, covered the village. So the villagers slept on. The sun climbed steadily ❹ until it reached the top of Maru. Then the shadow disappeared. ❺

When the sun's rays reached the village of Puaikura, Kapu woke up. ❻ He was not a lazy boy, but he did not want to wake before the sun. After a breakfast of coconut and breadfruit, he waded into the sparkling lagoon that ringed the island. ❼ There inside the protection of the coral walls, he swam, fished, and played with his friends. When the sun dipped low in the West, ❽ he brought home the four fish he had caught. ❾ Four fish never quite made the six people in his family full. ❿

Day after day, the same thing happened. The sun rose in the East. ⓫ The shadow of Maru covered the village. ⓬ At midday the sun reached the peak of the mountain ⓭ and chased the shadow away. ⓮ Then Kapu woke up. ⓯

For Kapu and his village this patten changed one dark night. Warriors from the nearby island of Aitutaki (AH-ee-too-tah-kee) paddled their double canoe ⓰ silently south. Under the cover of darkness the warriors landed on Rarotonga. "Shhh, do not wake the villagers," one said. ⓱ The warriors wanted to steal a mountain because their beautiful, coral island was flat. ⓲ A line of Aitutaki warriors snuck up the steep slopes of Maru. They grunted and puffed, *unh, puff-uff, unh, puff-uff.* ⓳ Surrounding the top of the mountain, ⓴ they stuck their spears into the stone. With their incredibly sharp spears, the astonishingly powerful warriors cut off the top of the mountain. Down the mountain side the men carried the peak, ㉑ *unh, puff-uff, unh, puff-uff.* When they reached their canoe, each held the mountain top over his head with one hand and paddled ㉒ with the other. When the warriors reached Aitutaki, they gently put the peak down and named it Maunga Pu (MAH-oon-gah POO), which means top of the mountain.

The next day the sun rose in the East as usual. ㉓ On Rarotonga, the shadow of Maru ㉔ still covered Puaikura. ㉕ But the mountain was shorter now. Much earlier than usual ㉖ the sun's rays reached the village. The shadow disappeared ㉗ and Kapu woke up. ㉘ He waded into the lagoon, ㉙ played with his friends, and caught eight fish. ㉚ Kapu still had time to admire the coral, swim, and lie on the beach before the sun dipped into the western seas. ㉛

When Kapu got home, he found that the Ariki, ㉜ or chief of the village, had called a meeting. ㉝ The villagers stared sadly at the strange, flat top of Maru. "Shall we follow the Aitutaki warriors?" the Ariki asked.

A warrior spoke up, ㉞ "How will we carry the mountain top? It would sink our canoes."

"We need our mountain back!" said another. ㉟

Then Kapu's mother spoke, ㊱ "Today my son brought home eight fish, instead of four. Today my daughters and I wove a full mat, instead of half a mat. The days are now longer for our village." There were mumbles of agreement.

"Hmmm." The Ariki thought a moment, then spoke, "We will let the Aitutaki warriors have the peak. From now on we will call our mountain Raemaru (RAH-ay-mah-roo), the empty shadow." He lifted his staff. "Now we can weave more mats, catch more fish, and have more time for singing and dancing."

If you go to Aitutaki today, you can climb to the top of the small mountain top of Maunga Pu, which was stolen from Rarotonga. And if you stay at Puaikura, on Rarotonga, you can sleep just past dawn because the flat topped mountain of Raemaru casts a small shadow. But the big shadow that let Kapu sleep away most of the day is now gone.

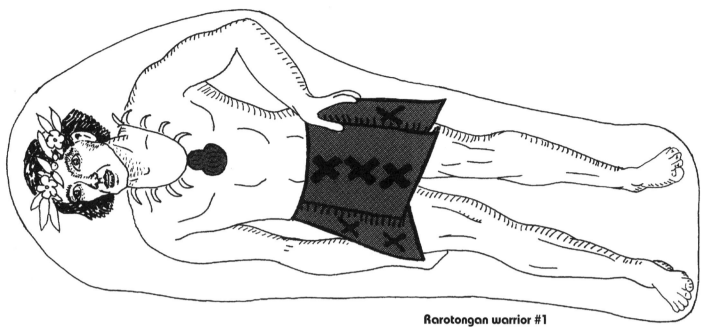

Rarotongan warrior #1

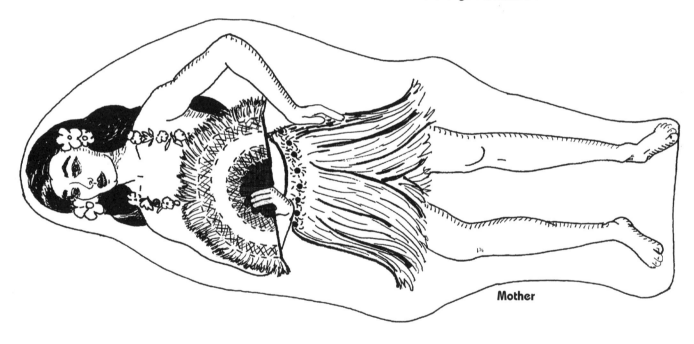

Mother

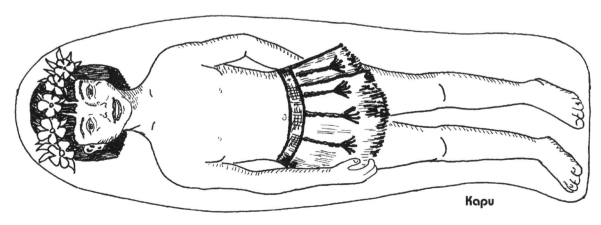

Kapu

Characters for Empty Shadow

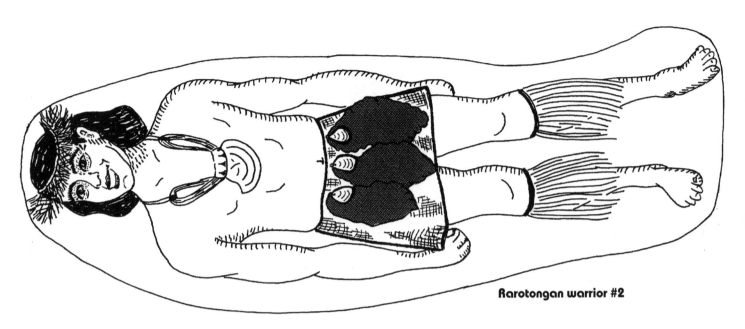

Rarotongan warrior #2

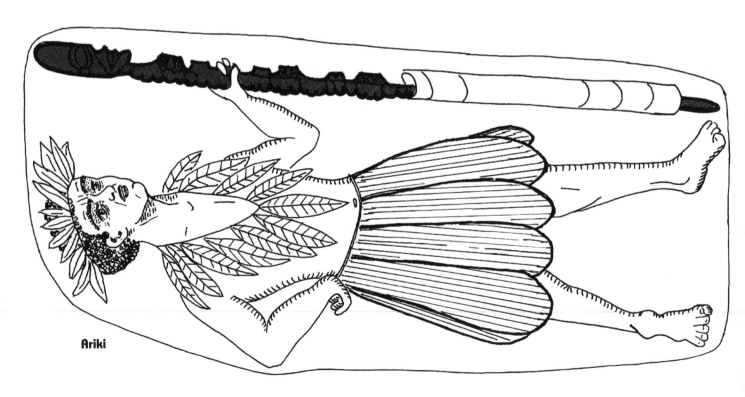

Ariki

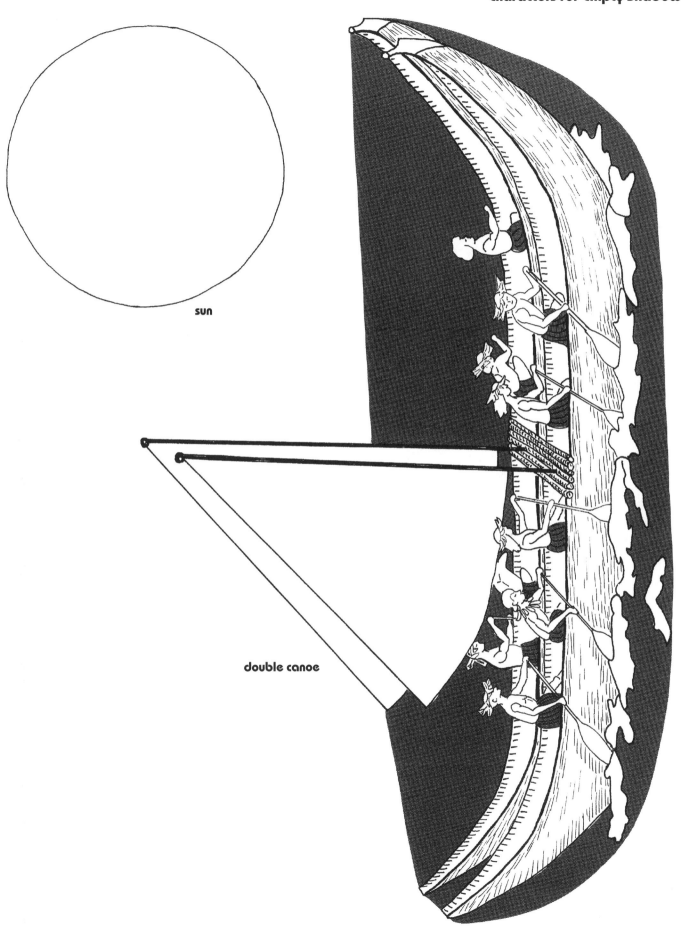

sun

double canoe

Characters for Empty Shadow

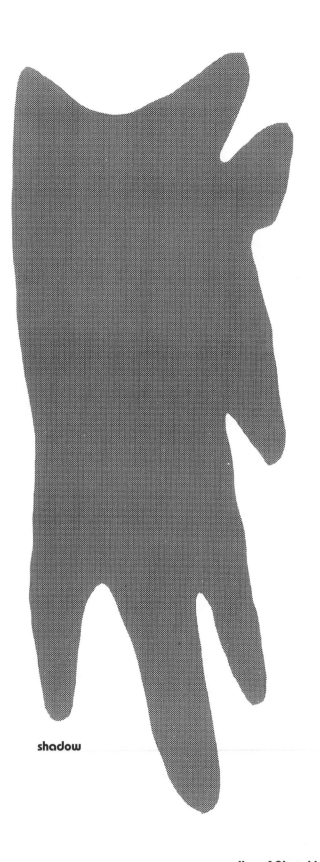

shadow

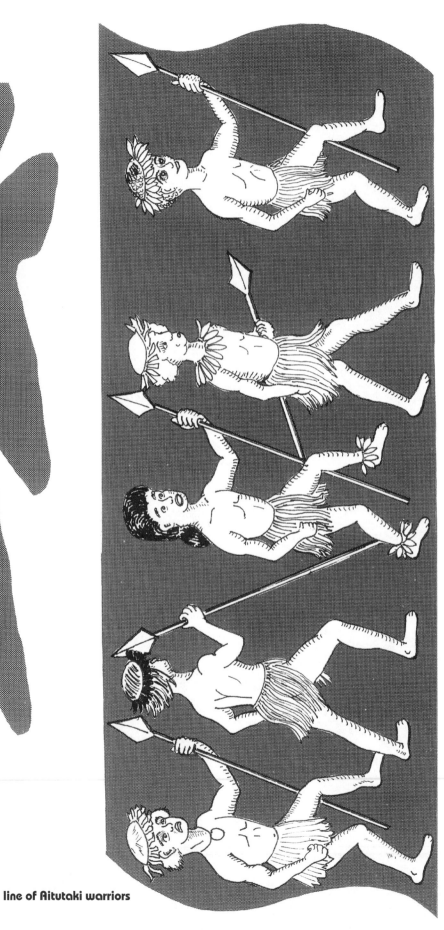

line of Aitutaki warriors

Movements of Felt Characters

For this story, position your felt board with the longer side horizontal. All left and right directions assume you are facing the front of the board.

Before beginning the story, take a minute to visualize the setting. This will help you understand where to place the felt pieces. Imagine a peaked mountain covering the right half of the felt board. The lagoon is at the far left of the board. To the right of the lagoon is the shoreline, and further right at the base of the mountain is the village of Puaikura. Most of the action in the story will take place in the left half of the board near the lagoon, shoreline, and village. In the right half of the board is the mountain peak and the eastern horizon near the board's right edge. Once you know where these locations are on your board, the movements of the characters become easy.

Begin the story with the board empty.

❶ Place the sun on the right side of the board on the eastern horizon about midway between the top and bottom of the board.

❷ Point to a spot left of center that you have chosen for the village of Puaikura.

❸ Add the shadow to the spot.

❹ Move the sun up in an arc ending at the mountain peak.

❺ Remove the shadow.

❻ Put Kapu in the village.

❼ Move Kapu several inches to the left so he is in the lagoon.

❽ Take the sun from the top and slide it in an arc to the left side of the board.

❾ Move Kapu to the right, out of the water, and into the village.

❿ Remove Kapu from the board.

⓫ Slip the sun off the left side and put it on the right edge.

⓬ Add the shadow over the village.

⓭ Move the sun in an arc to the mountain peak.

⓮ Take off the shadow.

⓯ Place Kapu in the village. Before beginning the next paragraph, remove Kapu and the sun. The board should now be empty.

⓰ Add the canoe on the lower left side of the board.

⓱ Remove the canoe.

⓲ Add the line of Aitutaki Warriors near the shoreline.

⓳ Move the line of warriors at a 45 degree angle up the left side of the imaginary mountain, continuing the grunts and puffs until they reach the top.

⓴ Put the line of warriors horizontally several inches from the top of the board, as if they were surrounding the peak.

㉑ Move the line of warriors back down the left side of the mountain. Continue the grunts and puffs until they reach the lower left corner.

㉒ Take the line of warriors off the board. Replace them with the canoe, which drifts to the left and off the board. The board is now empty.

You may have a literal child whose imagination cannot turn the warriors around as they descend the mountain or paddle back home. If he asks, just tell him you think that maybe it is easier to carry a mountain backwards.

㉓ Position the sun at the right side of the board.

24 Point to the village.

25 Cover the village with the shadow.

26 Move the sun in an arc and stop before the spot where the peak once was.

27 Remove the shadow.

28 Place Kapu in the village.

29 Slide Kapu to the left into the lagoon.

30 Put Kapu back to the right, out of the water.

31 Move the sun in an arc to the left side of the board.

32 Put the Ariki, the man who is carrying a staff, to the left of Kapu.

33 Add two warriors and his mother to the right of Kapu.

34 Point to one warrior. Point to the other warrior at 35 and Kapu's mother at 36.

The story ends with the Ariki, Kapu, two warriors, and his mother clustered in the village.

Second Activity Using Characters

The Riddling Princess: A Riddle Story

Use only the woman, the two Rarotongan warriors, and the Ariki in this riddle or guessing game. Set up your riddling story by saying, "There once was a beautiful princess who loved riddles. **(Place the woman on the board.)** Three handsome warriors wanted to marry her. **(Add the three men.)** So she decided to ask them riddles to help her decide which man to marry. The man who could answer the most riddles would make her happy and be her husband."

Proceed by asking riddles and letting the children help the warriors with the answers. When a warrior misses a riddle, remove him from the board until only one warrior is left. You then announce, "He has won the hand of the princess, and they lived happily ever after sharing riddles together."

You can make up riddles as you play. For the youngest listeners, narrow the category. For example, let the children know that the answer is an animal. Then ask, "It is gray, has big ears, and a trunk. What is it?"

Riddles can also be found in books. Two nursery rhymes that are riddles are "Humpty Dumpty" (egg) and "Little Nanny Etticoat" (candle). I have listed some good riddle books below.

What Am I? Very First Riddles by Stephanie Calmenson. New York: Harper, 1989. Easiest.

It Does Not Say Meow and Other Animal Riddle Rhymes by Beatrice De Regniers. New York: Clarion, 1972. Easy.

This Can Lick a Lollipop: Body Riddles for Kids by Joel Rothman. Garden City, New York: Doubleday, 1979. Easy, with words in English and Spanish.

Ten Copycats in a Boat: And Other Riddles edited by Alvin Schwartz. New York: Harper, 1988. Intermediate.

Riddles to Tell Your Cat by Caroline Levine. Morton Grove, Ill.: Whitman, 1992. Intermediate.

Macho Nacho and Other Rhyming Riddles, by Giulio Maestro. New York: Dutton, 1994. More difficult.

Creative Activities

Guessing Game: Bone Game

This is an American Indian game originally played with bones. Use two sticks of the same length. Make a mark near the end of one stick. Shuffle the sticks behind your back. Let the children guess which one has the mark.

Science Activity: Feel the Objects

Gather various objects that the American Indians used in their everyday life. Let the children look at and feel the objects and guess how the Indians used them. The Plains Indians used feathers for decorating baskets and bonnets.

The Pueblo Indians made bowls from clay. Indians of the Southwest used adobe, a mixture of clay, grass, and water, to make bricks to build their houses. Woodland Indians made homes from bark and logs. Indian corn was a crop the Wanpanoag Indians taught the Pilgrims how to use. Many Indians used sharp stones for cutting or making arrowheads. Buckskin or deer hide was used for clothing.

Ask questions about how an object feels. Is it soft, smooth, or sharp? Is it strong or delicate? Does something else feel similar?

Art Activity: Make a Paper Lei

To make a paper lei you will need yarn, sharp scissors, cellophane tape, and several colors of tissue paper. Plan to make about eight flowers for each lei. To make the flowers cut four inch squares from red, yellow, and pink tissue paper. With sharp scissors you can cut many layers of tissue at a time. Fold the squares in quarters, then fold one more time to make a triangle so that all folds bisect the center of the square. The center of the square will be the center of the flower. Cut a curve through all layers from the point at the longest edge of the triangle to about an inch from the flower center on the other edge. Unfold the paper. You now have a four petaled flower. Next, make slits to string the flowers on the yarn by folding the flowers in half and snipping two small cuts each a quarter inch from the center of the fold.

Cut a 36-inch piece of yarn for each lei. Wrap cellophane tape around one end of each piece of yarn to form a needle. You will need less than one inch of tape per child. Let the children string the flowers by threading the needle in one slit and out the other. The flowers should start and end about five inches from the yarn's end. After the children string the flowers, tie the two ends of the yarn together. The paper lei is finished.

The people of Rarotonga call these leis *ei kaki* (AY-ee KAH-kee) and welcome people to their island with them. Their greeting is *kia orana* (KEE-ah oh-RAH-nah). Hawaiians also put a lei over their visitor's necks and say, "Aloha" (ah-LOH-hah). Let the children practice saying kia orana and aloha.

Resources for Story Time

Poems

"If I Had a Paka" by Charlotte Pomerantz. From *If I Had a Paka*. New York: Greenwillow, 1982.

An animal poem in Swahili and English.

"Toy Tik Ka" by Charlotte Pomerantz. From *If I Had a Paka*. New York: Greenwillow, 1982.

A food poem in English and Vietnamese.

Books

Borreguita and the Coyote by Verna Aardema. New York: Knopf, 1991.

A Mexican folktale about a little lamb who outwits the coyote who wants to eat her. With large groups, details in the illustrations will be difficult to see.

Here Comes the Cat! by Frank Asch and Vladimir Vagin. New York: Scholastic, 1989.

A book in English and Russian about a visit from the cat. Be sure to let the children say, "Here Comes the Cat" in English. Let them try it in Russian too, pronounced syu-DAH ee-DYOT KOT.

Father's Rubber Shoes by Yumi Heo. New York: Orchard, 1995.

Yungsu who has recently moved to America misses his friends in Korea until he begins to make new friends.

Two of Everything by Lily Toy Hong. Morton Grove, Ill.: Whitman, 1993.

A humorous Chinese folktale about a pot that duplicates what falls into it.

Mama, Do You Love Me? by Barbara M. Joose. San Francisco:Chronicle, 1991.

In this simple tale, an Eskimo mother tells her child of her love.

Anansi and the Moss-Covered Rock by Eric Kimmel. New York: Holiday, 1988.

The ingredients in the story are a magic rock and the African mischief-maker, Anansi the spider.

Masai and I by Virginia Kroll. New York: Macmillan, 1992.

A young, African-American girl compares her life with what it might have been if she had been born in Africa.

Zomo the Rabbit by Gerald McDermott. San Diego: Harcourt, 1992.

A West African folktale about a rabbit who attempts three impossible tasks to earn wisdom.

Dream Catcher by Audrey Osofsky. New York: Orchard, 1992.

A Native American legend explaining an object that catches bad dreams. Thus, a child with one has only sweet dreams.

Momotaro, The Peach Boy by Linda Shute. New York: Lothrop, 1986.

A boy, who was found inside a peach, grows to fight an evil monster. Japanese folktale.

Nine O'Clock Lullaby by Marilyn Singer. New York: Harper Collins, 1991.

A concept book about what children are doing around the world when it is nine P.M. in Brooklyn.

Chato's Kitchen by Gary Soto. New York: Putnam, 1995.

Chato the cat lures the new mice family to his home for a feast in this slightly longer story sprinkled with Spanish words.

The House That Jack Built illustrated by Jenny Stow. New York: Dial, 1992.

The cumulative nursery rhyme is set in the Caribbean.

Music

"Jambo" and "Pole Pole." Cassette source: *Jambo and Other Call-and-Response Songs and Chants* by Ella Jenkins. Washington, D.C.: Smithsonian Folkways, 1990.

> *Jambo* means "hello" in Swahili and *pole* means "go slow." Children will enjoy both call-and-response songs.

"Anansi." Cassette source: *The Corner Grocery Store*, words by Bert Simpson, music by Raffi. Willowdale, Ont.: Troubador, 1979.

> A short ballad about Anansi, the traditional African spider/man. Good to use with an Anansi story.

5. Gifts

Introduction

Children love to receive and give gifts. Just mention the words "gift" or "present" to a group of children and everyone will have something to tell you. This chapter is about gifts, both concrete and intangible. The theme would be fun to use near the winter holidays of Christmas and Hanukkah when gift-giving is prevalent but a storytime on gifts can be used any time of year.

In the story "Teddy Bear," Maria's mother has given Maria a teddy bear. When Maria asks why it is called a teddy bear, Mama tells her the story of how these stuffed bears were named after Theodore Roosevelt. This story is historically accurate.

Before telling the story, spend a few minutes talking about names. When a baby is born, he or she is given a name by someone often a parent or grandparent. When new things are invented or made, someone chooses a name for it. This is a story about how a toy got its name.

Felt Board Story

Teddy Bear

Under the shiny, red paper which covered the tempting present, Maria found a teddy bear. She gave Mama a thank-you hug.❶

"I'm glad you like it," Mama said. "What will you name it?"

"I don't know." Maria rubbed the silky fur against her cheek. "Mama, why do we call it a teddy bear?" she asked.

"Just cuddle up here with me, and I'll tell you," Mama said. As they rocked, the chair murmured, *creak-an'-a-crick, creak-an'-a-crick.* ❷ "A long time ago, back in 1901, the Vice-President of the United States was a man named Theodore Roosevelt. ❸ His nickname was Teddy. He was an outdoors man who loved nature and animals. When President McKinley was killed, Theodore Roosevelt became the 26th President." *Creak-an'-a-crick, creak-an'-a-crick* , sang the rocker. ❹

"But what about the teddy bear?" Maria asked.

"I'm getting to that, Honey. ❺ A year later, when President Roosevelt wanted to relax, he went on a hunting trip to a wilderness area in Mississippi. ❻ On the banks of the Little Sunflower River, Roosevelt and six friends set up a camp of three sleeping tents and a food tent. With them was Holt Collier, an African American who had been a scout in the Civil War and was a famous bear hunter. Collier was in charge of the dogs who would track the bears. Then the men on horseback would follow the dogs.

"On the first day the men tracked a bear ❼ who led them through dense underbrush for a long while. Then the bear disappeared. ❽ The riders split into several groups but found no bear. Much later, Collier blew his horn to call the scattered hunting party. *Ta-doo! Ta-doo!* Roosevelt rode through the ash, oak, and cypress trees until he found Collier with a large bear tied to a tree. ❾ Collier had clubbed the bear with his rifle when it attacked the dogs. The men urged Roosevelt to shoot the bear. He refused. When his vacation ended four days later, Roosevelt still had failed to shoot a bear.

"Soon stories about the hunting trip were passed from person to person. A famous cartoonist named Clifford Berryman heard the stories and drew two cartoons about the incident called 'Drawing the Line in Mississippi.' In some of the stories and cartoons, things got a little mixed-up and the bear became a cute bear cub. ❿ Stories and the cartoon were printed in the *Washington Post*, and people everywhere saw them ." ⓫

Maria asked, "Was President Roosevelt angry?"

"No," Mama continued. "He didn't mind the teasing. He saw the humorous side of his unsuccessful bear hunt. Friends sent him miniature bears of every kind as a joke.

"Before long, a toy company began making plush bear cubs, ⓬ calling them 'Teddy bears,' after the bear that Teddy Roosevelt refused to shoot."

"Did he like having a toy named for him?"

"He didn't mind; although he couldn't see how his name would help the plush bear business. Since then, children everywhere call their cuddly, plush bears teddy bears. But, Maria, you can call yours anything you like."

They rocked gently as the chair whispered, *creak-an'-a-crick, creak-an'-a-crick.* ⓭ Suddenly Maria jumped up, "Come along, Theodore bear, let me show you my room."

Mother and Maria in rocker

Characters for Teddy Bear

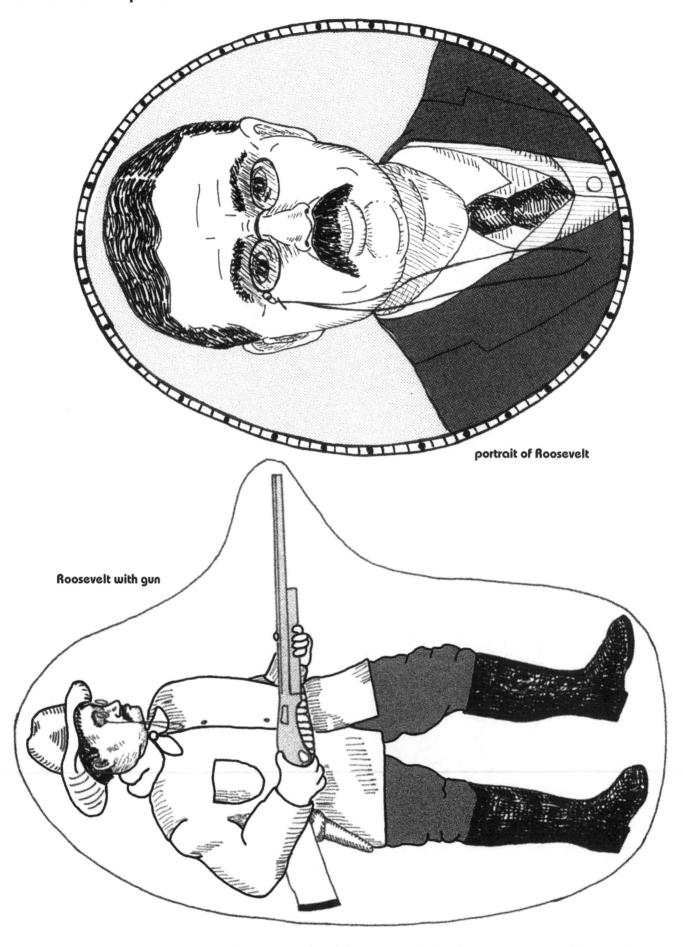

portrait of Roosevelt

Roosevelt with gun

bear cub

large bear

Characters for Teddy Bear

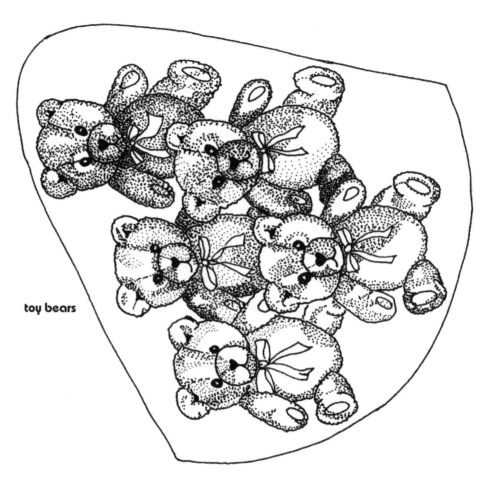

toy bears

newspaper reader

Movements of Felt Characters

Moving the felt characters for this story is easy since there is little interaction between the seven pieces. Before beginning, turn the felt board so the longer side is horizontal. Left and right directions assume you are facing the front of the board.

Start the story with the mother and her daughter in the rocking chair on the lower left corner of the board.

❶ Hug your arms across your chest.

❷ Each time you say, "*Creak-an'-a-crick*," rock back and forth to imitate the motion of a rocking chair.

❸ Add the portrait of Theodore Roosevelt above and to the right of the rocker.

❹ Rock back and forth.

❺ Remove the portrait.

❻ Place the hunting Roosevelt above and to the right of the rocker.

❼ Position the large bear to the right of Roosevelt.

❽ Remove the bear.

❾ Add the bear to the right of hunting Roosevelt.

❿ Remove the bear and place the bear cub in its spot.

⓫ Put the person reading the newspaper above and to the right of the bear cub.

⓬ Put the toy bears above and to the right of the newspaper.

⓭ Rock back and forth to the words *creak-an'-a-crick.*

The story ends with the rocker in the lower left corner. Above and to the right is the hunting Roosevelt facing the bear cub. One step up and to the right is the newspaper. In the upper right are the toy Teddy bears.

Second Activity Using Characters

Sequencing

This activity is a game using the important pre-reading skill of sequencing. When children can arrange events in appropriate order, it proves that they understand the causes and effects of the actions. The story "Teddy Bear" is not told in strict chronological order but as a flashback.

After sharing the story with the children, ask them if Maria could have received a Teddy bear before they were ever named or manufactured. In random order give them the following events, each linked to a felt piece:

Theodore Roosevelt becomes the 26th President (**oval portrait**).

President Roosevelt goes hunting (**man with rifle**).

He sees a bear in the woods (**large bear**).

A cartoon about his hunting is in the newspaper (**newspaper**).

Teddy bears are manufactured (**toy bears**).

Maria names her toy bear (**rocker**).

Ask the children to put the felt pieces in chronological order, from left to right.

If the children are too young for the above game, have them choose which come first and which is second in the events in the following sentences:

A bear cub (**cub**) grows up (**large bear**).

A mama bear (**large bear**) has a cub (**cub**).

Teddy bears are made (**teddies**) then a mother buys one for her daughter (**rocker**).

Creative Activities

Holiday Game: Mexican Piñata

Buy or make a piñata (a decorated, paper-mâché container filled with candies, small toys, or other gifts). Hang the piñata from a tree limb or ceiling. Then let one blindfolded child at a time swing a stick and try to break the piñata. When the piñata is broken, candy and gifts will fall to the ground, and the children can scramble for fistfuls of goodies. This game is played in Mexico, especially at Christmas time. To make the game safer, have an adult break the piñata and the children race to pick up the gifts. Be sure to hold some treats back for the timid.

Art Activity: Make Wrapping Paper

Cut sponges into various shapes. Have the children dip them in shallow pans of thinned paint, then press the sponges on large rolls of plain paper. After the paper dries, roll it, and you have designer wrapping paper.

Gift for the Birds: Make a Bird Feeder

Tie a string to a pine cone. Roll the cone in peanut butter, then in birdseed. Put this gift for the birds in a plastic bag for the children to take home and hang in a tree near a window. Then, they can watch the birds enjoy the gift.

Give an Intangible Gift: Sing a Song

Some of the most precious gifts are intangible gifts that cost no money. Children delight in giving and have few resources. Instead of buying presents, they can give hugs, help with a task, give a piece of their artwork, or sing a song to cheer someone's day.

Teach the group a short song such as "Old MacDonald Had a Farm," "I'm a Little Teapot," or "Where is Thumbkin?" Then give a gift of song by having the group sing the tune for a person or another group; a class, a teacher, a friend, or their parents.

Cassette resource for all three songs: *Wee Sing* by Pamela Beall and Susan Nipp. Los Angeles: Price Stern Sloan, 1981. Written music resource for all three songs: *Singing Bee!* compiled by Jane Hart. New York: Lothrop, 1982.

Resources for Story Time

Poems

"The Elephant," by Louis Phillips. From *A Zooful of Animals*, edited by William Cole. Boston: Houghton, 1992.

This short poem about wrapping an elephant has a wonderful large picture.

"Teddy Bear," a traditional rhyme done with motions.

Teddy bear, Teddy bear, turn all around.
Teddy bear, Teddy bear, touch the ground.
Teddy bear, Teddy bear, show your shoe.
Teddy bear, Teddy bear, that will do.
Teddy bear, Teddy bear, reach down low.
Teddy bear, Teddy bear, touch your toe.
Teddy bear, Teddy bear, turn out the light.
Teddy bear, Teddy bear, say, "Good night."

Books

Happy Birthday, Moon by Frank Asch. Englewood Cliffs, N.J.: Prentice Hall, 1982.

Bear tries to exchange gifts with the moon.

Dear Zoo by Rod Campbell. New York: Four Winds, 1982.

The zoo sends a variety of animals to a little boy until the right one is found in this lift-the-flap book. Simple and short.

Ask Mr. Bear by Marjorie Flack. New York: Macmillan, 1960.

Danny searches for the perfect, birthday gift for his mother until Mr. Bear suggests a bear hug.

Rata-Pata-Scata-Fata by Phillis Gershator. Boston: Little Brown, 1994.

On a Caribbean island Junjun wishes his chores away. Serendipitous events, like unexpected gifts, make his wishes come true.

Giving by Shirley Hughes. Cambridge, Mass.: Candlewick, 1993.

A simple book exploring the many aspects of giving.

New Shoes for Silvia by Johanna Hurwitz. New York: Morrow, 1993.

Silvia receives a pair of red shoes from her Aunt Rosita and finds clever uses for the shoes until she grows into them. Latin American setting. Beautifully illustrated by Jerry Pinkney.

Best Present by Holly Keller. New York: Greenwillow, 1989.

A little girl tries to give her hospitalized grand- mother a present.

Two Travelers by Christopher Manson. New York: Holt, 1990.

The Caliph of Baghdad sends Isaac to the Emperor of France with a gift, an elephant!

Love from Uncle Clyde by Nancy Parker. New York: Dodd, Mead, 1977.

Uncle Clyde sends the unusual gift of a hip- popotamus.

Angel Child, Dragon Child by Michele Maria Surat. Milwaukee: Raintree, 1983.

A Vietnamese girl makes a friend who suggests the school have a fair to raise money to bring her mother to American, the best gift of all.

Rainbow Crow retold by Nancy Van Laan. New York: Knopf, 1989.

The crow brings the gift of fire to the animals. A legend of the North American Indians.

Something Special for Me by Vera Williams. New York: Greenwillow, 1991.

Rosa cannot decide what she wants for her birthday until she hears an accordion.

Follow the Drinking Gourd by Jeanette Winter. New York: Knopf, 1988.

Peg Leg Joe teaches slaves a song, which tells them the path to freedom. One family escapes by following the stars north in this longer, picture story. Music to the song is included.

Mr. Rabbit and the Lovely Present by Charlotte Zolotow. New York: Harper & Row, 1962.

Mr. Rabbit helps a little girl find a gift for her mother.

Music

"Gift Giving." Sing the following song to the tune of "The Mulberry Bush." Cassette source: *Playtime Parade* by Patti Dallas and Laura Baron. Yellow Springs, Ohio: Garden Glow Recording, 1989. Music source: *Jane Yolen's Mother Goose Songbook.* Honesdale, Pa.: Boyds Mill, 1992.

This is the way we give a gift,
Give a gift, give a gift.
This is the way we give a gift,
Always happily.

"Simple Gifts." Cassette source: *Songs for Sleepyheads and Out-of-Beds.* Victoria, B.C.: Lullaby Lady Productions, 1984. Music source: *Go in and out the Window* edited by Dan Fox. New York: Metropolitan Museum of Art, 1987.

Traditional Quaker song.

6. Winter Wonderland

Introduction

For children winter is a special time of year. They can go out and play in the snow or stay home by the firelight and listen to stories. Snow has a magical quality because it can steal in silently overnight and completely change the outside world.

The felt board story, "The Grotto Lunkers are Coming," is a tale set in a modern Alaskan village near Mt. McKinley. I have given the characters Eskimo names: Nukatpiagruk (NOOK-at-pee-a-grook) means boy; Inuk (EEN-ook), man. Grotto Lunkers are modern imaginary monsters, not ones linked to Eskimo or Athabascan legends. While this is a story of a snowy day, it is also about the power of stories and their ability to create and chase away fears.

This theme works well during any winter month. If you use it in early January, you may want to try the activities related to New Year's Day, Old and New and Discuss New Year's Day. Also one musical resource, "Chicken Soup with Rice," is about the twelve months in a year.

Felt Board Story

The Grotto Lunkers are Coming

Beneath the shadow of Denali, a great mountain in Alaska, Nukatpiagruk ❶ crunched through the snow in his warm parka and sealskin boots called mukluks. No villagers noticed Nukatpiagruk trudging through the snow ❷ toward the lonely pine. In his head whirled memories of the stories, singing, and dancing from last night's village gathering. Vaguely he remembered Inuk, the master storyteller, begin a story about Grotto Lunkers, hazy monsters who hide in mountain crevices. Nukatpiagruk wished he had not fallen asleep before the tale was finished.

He ❸ stopped at the lonely pine, which was covered with freshly fallen snow. A sharp wind brushed his cheek and he heard *shhh-flump*. *Shhh-flump*? he thought. *Shhh-flump*? What goes *shhh-flump*? He froze because maybe a Grotto Lunker goes *shhh-flump*. Maybe a Grotto Lunker was hiding behind the tree. Again Nukatpiagruk felt a swift gust followed by *shhh-flump*.

Nukatpiagruk turned. ❹ He crunched toward the village as quickly as his mukluks would allow. Inuk, the wise storyteller, would know what to do.

Along the way he met a moose. ❺ "I heard a *shhh-flump*," he said. "Do you think it was a Grotto Lunker?"

"Of course," said the moose. The moose let loose a hair-raising honk and trotted along with Nukatpiagruk toward the village. ❻

Nukatpiagruk and the moose crunched and trotted through the snow until they met a loping bear. ❼

"I heard *shhh-flump*," said Nukatpiagruk.

"Grotto Lunker," said the moose. "Do you think there is a whole pack of them?"

"Of course," said the bear. The bear let out a tizzy of a *grrr*, ❽ and Nukatpiagruk, the moose, and the grizzly bear crunched and trotted and loped through the snow until they met an eagle. ❾

"I head *shhh-flump*," said Nukatpiagruk.

"Grotto Lunker," said the moose.

"A whole pack of them," said the bear. "Do you think they are right behind us?"

"Of course," said the eagle.

Nukatpiagruk crunched, the moose trotted, the bear loped, and the eagle flapped through the snowy land until they reached the village.

Inuk ❿ greeted them with a smile. Patiently, he listened.

"At the lonely pine I heard *shhh-flump*," said Nukatpiagruk.

"Grotto Lunker," said the moose.

"A whole pack of them," said the bear.

"Right behind us," added the eagle.

Calmly, Inuk told them to stay where they were, that he would face the Grotto Lunkers alone. ⓫ At the lonely pine he heard *shhh-flump* as a pile of new snow slid from a branch and hit the drifts below. When he returned, his eyes danced like snowflakes.

"You will see no more Grotto Lunkers," he said. ⓬ "They are story creatures and returned home to where they belong, in stories."

Nukatpiagruk never did see any Grotto Lunkers. ⓭ But after that, on cold, winter days especially after a new snow he would hear *shhh-flump*. That sound would trigger a tingling feel like a persistent and pesky itch. Then, he would gather his friends and tell them the story of the day he set out toward the lonely pine, heard the Grotto Lunkers, and saved the village.

first Nukatpiagruk

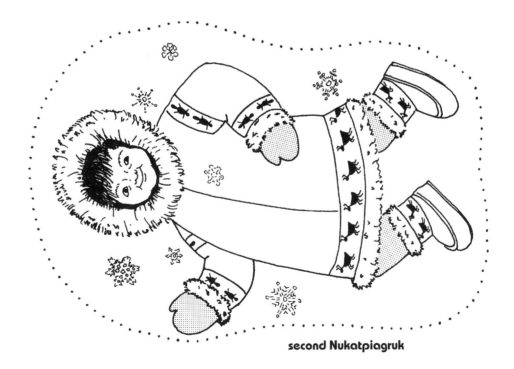

second Nukatpiagruk

Inuk the storyteller

lonely pine

moose

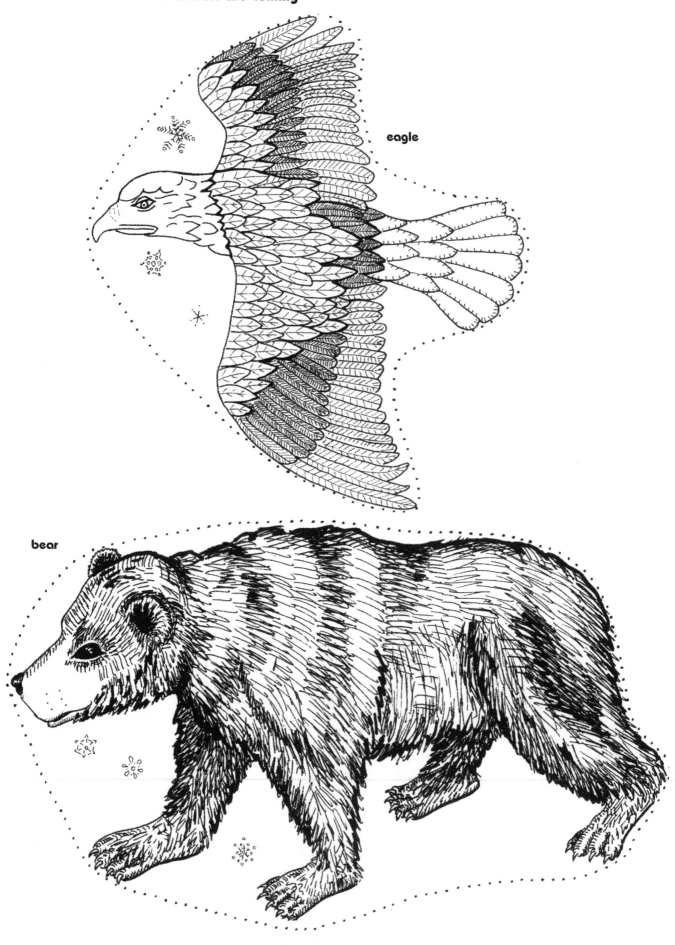

eagle

bear

Movements of Felt Characters

For this story turn your board so the longer sides are horizontal. The movements are easy because the characters generally move in a straight, horizontal line across the felt board. Mentally divide the straight line across the board into six sections. All left and right directions assume you are facing the front of the felt board.

Begin the story with the lonely pine in the right or sixth section, midway from the top and bottom. The tree remains in this position throughout the story.

❶ Place the Nukatpiagruk that faces right in the second section, on the same horizontal line as the tree.

❷ Move Nukatpiagruk halfway to the tree or to the fourth section.

❸ Put him next to the tree, in the fifth section.

❹ Remove right-facing Nukatpiagruk and add to the fourth section the Nukatpiagruk that is striding left. The first Nukatpiagruk will be used again at the end of the story.

❺ Place the moose in the fifth section.

❻ Move Nukatpiagruk then the moose one section to the left.

❼ There is now room to add the bear to section five.

❽ Move Nukatpiagruk, the moose, and the bear each one section to the left. Again, section five is empty.

❾ Put the eagle in section five, positioning it above the other animals and leaving space below for a character to be added later.

❿ Put Inuk in the first section so he faces Nukatpiagruk.

⓫ Place Inuk below the eagle in section five.

⓬ Remove Inuk.

⓭ Replace the left-striding Nukatpiagruk with the first Nukatpiagruk.

The story ends with Nukatpiagruk facing his three friends with the tree to the right.

Second Activity Using Characters

Memory Game

Name the pieces as you place them on the felt board: moose, bear, eagle, boy, and storyteller. Use "boy" and "storyteller" instead of "Nukatipiagruk" and "Inuk" to make it simpler for the children. Tell the children to look at the pictures, then close their eyes. Step in front of the felt board, since there is usually one child too curious not to peek, and remove one of the pictures. Tell them to open their eyes and guess which one is missing. Play the game several times removing a different picture each time.

Creative Activities

Language Development: Old and New

Bring a few items that are old and new such as shoes, tennis balls, toys. Compare pictures of old and new cars, people, and animals. Talk about how you can tell if things are old or new. Mention the values of both old and new things. For example, old shoes are comfortable. New shoes are often shiny.

Dramatic Play: Be a Snowflake

If possible, have the children watch snowflakes fall. Let them pretend they are snowflakes, falling from the sky, being blown by the wind, whirling around, landing on the ground, being rolled into a snowman. Inspire them with music such as the "Dance of the Sugarplum Fairy" from *The Nutcracker Suite*. Cassette source: *The Nutcracker* by Peter Tchaikovsky. New York: Allegro, 1980.

Skill Game: Stick in a Hoop

This is a simplified, noncompetitive version of a Native American game of skill. Make a circle about five feet in diameter on the floor using a rope or draw a circle in the snow. Find four sticks shorter than the diameter of the circle. Let the children take turns tossing the sticks and trying to get them inside the hoop. Give everyone a chance to try. Music appropriate to play during this game is "We are Native American Tribes" from *We Are America's Children* by Ella Jenkins. Washington, D.C.: Smithsonian Folkway Records, 1989.

Language Development: Discuss New Year's Day

Explain that New Year's Day is celebrated on January 1 in the United States. People often celebrate with parties, football games, and parades. Many people stay up the night before, called New Year's Eve, until the new year arrives at midnight. At midnight people often make loud sounds with noisemakers and horns. Many people also make plans to be a better person in the next year. These plans are called resolutions. Ask the children if they can think of any resolutions or plans for next year. Let the children pretend it is New Year's Eve. Give the children confetti and rhythm band instruments. Set an egg timer for a few minutes. When it rings, pretend it is midnight on New Year's Eve by throwing confetti, making noise with musical instruments, and shouting, "Happy New Year!"

Science Activity: Melting Snow

Bring inside two snowballs about four inches in diameter. Put them in a shallow pan. Watch them melt. What do they become? How much water is left? Discuss snow using the words "freezing temperature", "ice Crystals", and "melting". It took me about fifteen minutes to melt two snowballs yielding about 1/3 cup of water. Stories in the resource section about melting snow include *Snowball* and *The Snowy Day*.

Resources for Story Time

Poems

"Baby Bear Moon" by Joseph Bruchac and Jonathan London. From *Thirteen Moons on Turtle's Back*. New York: Philomel, 1992.

A poem from a Native American legend with a beautiful painting by Thomas Locker.

"Cold" by Shirley Hughes. From *Out and About*. New York: Lothrop, 1988.

A lively, full-page illustration appears before the poem, and a double spread of winter fun follows it.

"Winter Moon" by Langston Hughes. From *Sing a Song of Popcorn*. New York: Scholastic, 1988.

A lovely, two-page illustration accompanies the poem by the well-known African American writer.

Books

The Mitten retold and illustrated by Jan Brett. New York: Putnam, 1989.

Animals take refuge in a warm mitten. A Ukrainian tale.

Snow on Snow on Snow by Cheryl Chapman. New York: Dial, 1994.

A simple story of an African-American boy who loses then finds his dog while sledding.

Snowballs by Lois Ehlert. San Diego: Harcourt, 1995.

Collage illustrations of a snow family and the "good stuff" used to adorn them. Bold, bright and simple. A discussion of snow follows the brief story.

Snowy Day by Ezra Jack Keats. New York: Viking, 1962.

Peter, an African-American boy, enjoys a day in the snow.

What's Claude Doing? by Dick Gachenbach. New York: Clarion, 1984.

When Claude won't come out to play, the other animals worry.

Nessa's Fish by Nancy Luenn. New York: Atheneum, 1990.

> An Eskimo girl guards the fish when her grandmother becomes ill while they are ice fishing in the Arctic.

A Winter Place by Ruth Yaffe Radin. Boston: Little Brown, 1982.

> A family sets off to a frozen pond in the mountains. The detailed paintings demand a closer look.

Runaway Mittens by Jean Rogers. New York: Greenwillow, 1988.

> Pica, an Eskimo boy, loses his mittens. Then they turn up in odd places.

Three Bags Full by Ragnhild Scamell. New York: Orchard, 1993.

> Millie, a kindhearted sheep gives away her wool. What will happen to her when it snows?

A Hat for Minerva Louise by Janet Stoeke. New York: Dutton, 1994.

> Minerva Louise finds a pair of mittens, perfect for keeping both ends of this snow-loving hen warm.

Fox's Dream by Keizaburo Tejima. New York: Philomel, 1987.

> Lovely woodcuts by a Japanese master evoke the mood of a winter forest where a lonely fox finds his dream of companionship.

Music

"Frosty, the Snowman." Cassette source: *Raffi's Christmas Album.* Hollywood, Calif.: Shoreline, 1983. Music source: *Christmas Songs for Kids.* Milwaukee: Hal Leonard, 1992.

"Jingle Bells." Cassette source: *Raffi's Christmas Album.* Hollywood, Calif.: Shoreline, 1983. Music source: *Tom Glazer's Treasury of Songs for Children.* Garden City, New York: Doubleday, 1964.

"Chicken Soup with Rice." Song version of the book by Maurice Sendak. Cassette source: *Maurice Sendak Soundbook.* New York: Caedmon, 1981.

> A toe-tapping song that tours the months of the year. Sung by Carole King.

Video

The Snowman. New York: Random House Video, Snowman Enterprises, 1982.

> In this animated film, based on the book by Raymond Briggs, a snowman comes to life and escorts a boy to the North Pole. 28 min.

Snowplows at Work. Truckee, Calif.: Bill Aaron Productions, 1994.

> How snow removal equipment works. See a push plow, road grader, bucket loader, sanding truck, rotary blower, snow cat, and flanger. Meet the men and women who drive them. 26 min.

7. Animals We Love

Introduction

Animals, from big, floppy-eared elephants to small, long-tailed mice, fascinate children of all ages. They identify with animals especially the small, powerless ones in the stories they hear. Animal themes are popular with children, and this chapter has many kinds of animal characters for them to enjoy.

The felt board story, "Moonlight Mice: A Tale of Love," is an adventure about two mice who explore the forbidden territory of the Hall and fall in love. Since it is a love story and the felt pieces are red and white, it might be useful near Valentine's Day. A second activity uses the eleven mice to practice simple mathematics: counting forward and backward and simple addition and subtraction.

In this chapter I have listed poems, stories, songs, and videos about many animals that will delight young animal lovers. There are poems about a mouse, cow, fish, crow, horse, and frog. Owls, elephants, koalas, toads, coyotes, and cats star in the books. The music resources include two songs, one about a dog and the other about two crocodiles. The videos show rabbits and many other wild animals. These materials are especially appropriate for an audience with a wide age range such as family groups.

Felt Board Story

Moonlight Mice: A Tale of Love

Late one night when the moon was full, a daring mouse ❶ from the Living Room crossed the border into the forbidden Hall. First he trembled in the shadows, then skittered across the wooden floor to a throw rug beyond. ❷ Silvery moonlight passed through a small window and spotlighted the mouse on the rug. He looked right and left. He saw a bowl of red and pink carnations on a small table. He looked up and down. A mirror above the table multiplied the flowers. But he saw no monsters or any of the other evils that he'd been told were in the Hall.

"Eeek," he squeaked when he saw movement in a dim corner of the room. ❸

A voice as soft as a cloud whispered to him, "Who's there?"

"Wade," he said, "Prince of the mice of the Living Room. Who are you?"

"Wenda from the Kitchen. You are not a monster," she said.

As she moved into the light, ❹ he said, "Neither are you. You are pretty." They sat on the thick rug and talked until the moon disappeared and a pale light shone through the window. ❺

The next night, Wade ❻ and Wenda ❼ met again in the forbidden, moonlit Hall. They shared stories their elders had told them about the unknown evils they feared might be lurking in the Hall. "But I found nothing bad here," Wenda said, "I met a friend, and that was good." In the early morning they left to go home. When the moonlight glowed and they met again in the Hall, each had brought a friend. **8** Together they talked, played games, and danced. Soon, both invited more friends. **9** Wenda and Wade brought cheese and crackers and they had a joyous party.

Eventually, the elders found out. **10** The Living Room mice forbade their young mice to explore past their borders. The Kitchen mice posted a soldier **11** at the edge of their territory to keep their young mice at home.

One night the soldier yawned and fell asleep. **12** The young Kitchen mice **13** and the young Living Room mice **14** snuck into the hall to play together. The soldier awoke in the midst of a dance. **15** Since he saw no evil in the Hall and he loved parties, he joined in the fun. **16**

They danced and played and one by one returned home as the moonlight faded. **17**

The next day the soldier mouse **18** talked to the Kitchen Mouse King. **19** "Nothing bad," he said.

"Humph," said the King.

Prince Wade **20** tried to convince his mother, **21** the Queen of the Living Room mice, that the unknown land was not evil. "I found a friend there," he said.

"Humph," said the Queen.

Three days later both rulers finally agreed that the Hall was no longer forbidden land. **22** It became a playground, where young mice met, danced, and frolicked. Even the King and Queen had a good time there.

And as for Wenda **23** and Wade, **24** the first to explore the Hall **25** that night in the moonlight, they fell in love and lived happily ever after.

Wenda

Wade

red mouse friend

white mouse friend

Characters for Moonlight Mice

white mouse king

soldier

red mouse queen

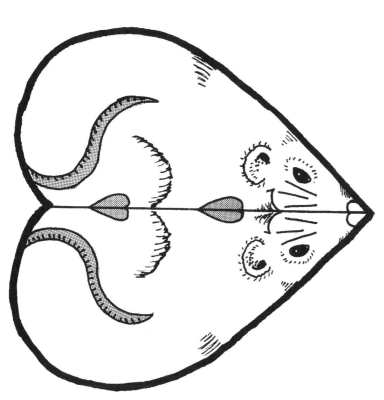

white half-heart mice

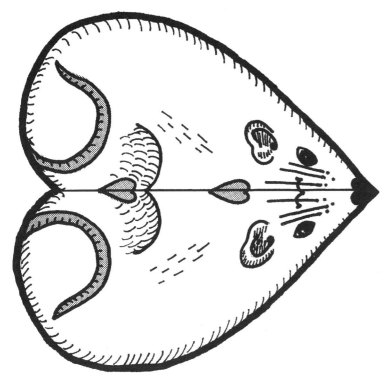

red half-heart mice

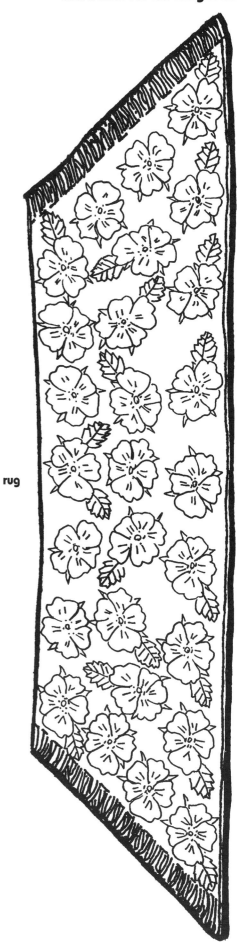

rug

Hints for Making Felt Characters

The Living Room mice should be red (Wade, the Queen, the skinny mouse, and the pair of half-heart shaped mice with black noses). The Kitchen mice should remain white (Wenda, the King, the soldier, the standing mouse, and the pair of half-heart shaped mice with white noses). The two colors of mice help the storyteller keep the mice going on and off the correct sides of the board. Color the roses on the rug red and pink. The clothing and other accessories on the mice can be any color, but using red, pink, and white for everything looks nice.

Cut around the black shapes that surround the mice. The most difficult pieces to cut out are the four mice that make the two hearts. Separate the pairs of half-heart shaped mice with one cut after you have glued the felt to them. This way the pairs will fit neatly together at the end of the story.

Movements of Felt Characters

Before the story begins position the longer side of the felt board horizontally. In the center about two-thirds of the way down, add the rug, which remains there until the end. Throughout the story move Wade (in the vest) and the red, Living Room mice on and off the right side of the felt board. Move Wenda (with the bow in her hair) and the white, Kitchen mice on and off the left side of the board. All directions assume you are facing the board.

❶ Place Wade on the board a couple of inches from the right edge.

❷ Put Wade above the right half of the rug.

❸ Add Wenda near the lower left corner.

❹ Move Wenda to the left half of the rug.

❺ Remove Wade and Wenda.

❻ Put Wade above the right side of the rug.

❼ Place Wenda above the left side of the rug.

❽ Add the skinny, red mouse and standing, white mouse, bringing them from their respective sides. Position Skinny to the left of Wenda. Place the standing white mouse to the right of Wade.

❾ Add the white, half-heart mouse which faces left and the red, half-heart mouse which faces right. Place them on either side of the rug facing center.

❿ Remove all mice from the board. Make sure the red mice are removed to the right; white, to the left. Simply pick up all the white mice and return them to the left side; then remove the red mice.

⓫ Put the white, soldier mouse near the left edge of the board.

⓬ Lay the soldier on his back, as if he were sleeping.

⓭ Scatter two, white half-heart mice, the standing white mouse, plus Wenda around the rug, as if they were partying.

⓮ Add three red mice (two half-heart mice and Skinny) plus Wade. Intermix them with the white mice.

⓯ Return the soldier mouse to an upright position.

⓰ Move the soldier mouse to any empty spot among the mice. Begin removing mice as you begin the sentence, "They danced and played and one by one…" until you have taken off all mice except the soldier mouse by number ⓱ . Be careful to take them to the correct side. Again, it is easier to remove one color at a time.

⓲ Move the soldier mouse near the lower left corner, leaving room for the King to his left.

⑲ Add the King in the cape so the two mice face each other.

⑳ Place Wade in the upper right corner.

㉑ Add the Queen to Wade's left.

㉒ Put the three white mice and three red mice around the felt board leaving the space above the rug empty.

㉓ Position Wenda above the rug's left side.

㉔ Position Wade over the rug's right side.

㉕ Pick up the two white, half-heart-shaped mice and fit them together to form a white heart above Wade. Then, make a heart from the two similar red mice and place it above Wenda.

The story ends with all felt pieces on the board.

Second Activity Using Characters

Ten Little Mice

Use ten of the eleven mice from the story. Add a mouse to the felt board as you count forward to the tune of "Ten Little Indians" using the following words:

> One little, two little, three little mice,
> Four little, five little, six little mice,
> Seven little, eight little, nine little mice,
> Ten little mice in the Hall.

Then count backward removing one mouse at a time using these words:

> Ten little, nine little, eight little mice,
> Seven little, six little, five little mice,
> Four little, three little, two little mice,
> One little mouse in the Hall.

When you repeat the poem, pause to let the children fill in the numbers. Or with a group that is shy, before you start ask, "How many?" and encourage them to sing along.

A good recorded source for the tune is the cassette *Wee Sing* by Pamela Beall and Susan Nipp. Los Angeles: Price Stern Sloan, 1981. The tune is listed under "Ten Little Fingers." A written music source is *Tom Glazer's Treasury of Songs for Children*, compiled by Tom Glazer. Garden City, New York: Doubleday, 1964.

For older children try some visual addition using mice visiting the forbidden Hall. For example:

> "2 little mice, plus 3 more dare. So how many mice are there, in the Hall?"

Simple subtraction can also be made into a game with the following words:

> "In the Hall there are 3 little mice. When 2 get a scare and scamper away, how many mice are there, in the Hall?"

Creative Activities

Language Game: Where Has My Little Dog Gone?

Repeat the nursery rhyme, "Oh Where, Oh Where Has My Little Dog Gone?" Use a small picture or replica of a dog and hide it under various objects like a cup, book, napkin, hat, or mitten. Let the children guess where the dog is hidden but only by telling you verbally where they think it might be. No pointing and no touching.

Art Activity: Make a Pasta Snake

First, let each child paint twelve pieces of rigatoni and one piece of straight macaroni with poster paint. Painting all sides is easier if rigatoni is held on a pencil or small stick and macaroni is on a short, twist tie.

After the pasta dries, take a yard of string for each snake. To prevent the string from fraying during stringing, wrap a small piece of tape around one end.

Let the children put one rigatoni on the string. Tie the string so the rigatoni will not slip off. Tuck the short end of the string inside the pasta bead. Have them string the rest of the rigatoni, then one macaroni at the end. Tie the string around the macaroni, then push the macaroni inside the last rigatoni like a stopper. The children will enjoy slinking the pasta snake across the floor or a table by pulling the remaining string.

Physical Activity: Walk like the Animals

Choose an animal; then have everyone walk across the room like that animal. Walk back like another animal. Try elephant, duck, lion, crab, snake, dog, cat, cow, frog, chicken, turtle, and rabbit. Encourage creative approaches.

Observation Game: Who's There?

Before the activity session find large pictures of animals cut from old calendars or magazines. Cover the pictures with self-stick removable notes. The pictures should be letter paper size or larger; the notes, less than two by four inches.

In front of the children hold up a picture covered with notes. Remove one adhesive note at a time until the children can guess what the animal is. After removing all the notes from the guessed picture, start over with another animal picture.

Resources for Story Time

Poems

"Hickory Dickory Dock." From *The Real Mother Goose*. Chicago: Rand McNally, 1916.

This nursery rhyme works well as a stretch. Begin with one arm overhead. Run the fingers of your other hand up your body and arm pretending your hand is a mouse. When you say, "One," clap both hands overhead, then run your fingers down your arm.

Cassette source: *Wee Sing* by Pamela Beall and Susan Nipp. Los Angeles: Price Stern Sloan, 1981. This musical version counts to four.

"This Little Cow Eats Grass." From *Chinese Mother Goose Rhymes*, edited by Robert Wyndham. Cleveland: World Publishing, 1968.

A Chinese nursery rhyme with a nice illustration by Ed Young.

"Leaping Flying Fish," "Detestable Crow," "Galloping Pony," and "Little Frog." From *Red Dragonfly on My Shoulder*, Haiku translated by Sylvia Cassedy and Kunihiro Suetake. New York: HarperCollins, 1992.

Molly Bang illustrates these Japanese poems with collages of unusual objects including a yam, potato chips, a clam shell, a gull feather, a rock, and buttons.

Books

My Cat Jack by Patricia Casey. Cambridge, Mass.: Candlewick, 1994.

A brief look at a cat stretching, pouncing, licking, and purring.

After the nonfictional story, lead the children in imitating Jack by yawning, stretching down, stretching up, curling, and lapping.

Koala Lou by Mem Fox. San Diego: Harcourt, 1988.

A little koala wants her mother to say, "Koala Lou, I do love you!" so she enters the Bush Olympics. Australian.

Cat Goes Fiddle-i-fee by Paul Galdone. New York: Clarion, 1985.

Each time you say, "And the cat goes," have the children raise their arms from the elbows and finish your sentence with "Fiddle-i-fee." An American folk song.

If Anything Ever Goes Wrong at the Zoo by Mary Hendrick. San Diego: Harcourt, 1993.

In this delightful romp Leslie invites the animals to her house if there is trouble at the zoo.

Toad Is the Uncle of Heaven by Jeanne Lee. New York: Holt, 1985.

Toad goes to the King of Heaven to ask for rain. Vietnamese folktale.

Puss in Boots by Charles Perrault. Retold by Linda Cauley. San Diego: Harcourt, 1986.

Short version of the French fairy tale of the clever cat who wins wealth and a princess for his master.

Two by Two by Barbara Reid. New York: Scholastic, 1992.

The rhyming song about Noah and the animals illustrated in bas-relief with modeling paste. Music to the song is in the back of the book.

Sam Who Never Forgets by Eve Rice. New York: Greenwillow, 1977.

Sam feeds the zoo animals every day, but poor elephant is hungry.

Coyote Steals the Blanket retold by Janet Stevens. New York: Holiday, 1993.

A Ute legend about coyote who refuses to give up a blanket that does not belong to him.

Owl Babies by Martin Waddell. Cambridge, Mass.: Candlewick, 1992.

Three baby owls wake up to find Owl Mother gone. A short and sweet story with bold ink and watercolor drawings by Patrick Benson.

Music

"Bingo." Cassette source: *Turkey in the Straw with Phil Rosenthal.* Silver Spring, Md.: American Melody, 1985. Music source: *Go in and out the Window,* edited by Dan Fox. New York: Metropolitan Museum of Art, 1987.

A traditional song from Maryland about a dog named Bingo.

"Deux Cocodries," Cassette source: *Le Hoogie Boogie.* Cambridge, Mass.: Rounder, 1992.

A lively song and game in Cajun French from Louisiana. Sung by Michael "Beausoleil" Doucet and family. In the game two children march around to the music. Each time "*Si les cocodries*" is sung, the marching children point to another child who joins them as the crocodile's tail. Continue the game until everyone is slithering along to the music.

Videos

"Tale of Peter Rabbit." From *The Tale of Mr. Jeremy Fisher and the Tale of Peter Rabbit.* Read by Meryl Streep. New York:Rabbit Ear Productions, 1987.

A way to share Beatrix Potter's classic tale with many children at once. 15 min.

Bear Cubs, Baby Ducks, and Kooky Kookaburras by Bruce Somers Jr. and Caroline Sommers. Burbank, Calif.: Columbia Tristar Home Video a Lost Kitty Production for the National Geographic Society, 1994.

A mix of puppets, cartoons, and live animal footage to quench a child's curiosity. With songs, poems, and music the video shows baby wood ducks, stingrays, kookaburras, penguins, alligators, seahorses, Kodiak bears, zebras, springboks, sea turtles, and more. Too long to be part of a story time, but great for a follow-up activity or part of a theme week. 33 min.

8. Color Gallery

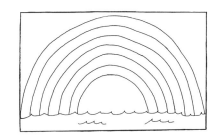

Introduction

Children marvel at the wonderful colors in the world around them. They enjoy looking at colors, comparing hues, and creating artwork with splashes of colors. Ask a group of children what their favorite color is, and most will have a decided opinion. The story in this chapter is set in Puerto Rico where Belinda wants to paint the perfect picture for her *Abuelita* (ah-BWEH-lee-tah), the Spanish word for Grandma. In "Picture for Abuelita" Belinda tries to decide which colors to take with her to paint this picture. If enough of the children in your group know Spanish, read both the English and Spanish names for the colors. Both languages are written on the tubes of paint.

The second activity with the felt characters is a memory game using the primary and secondary colors: red, orange, yellow, green, blue, and purple. In this chapter, I have used these six colors. In physics, however, the colors in the rainbow spectrum are called red, orange, yellow, green, blue, and violet. Most children are more familiar with the word "purple" than with "violet," since their basic crayon box contains purple. Thus, I have used the pigment color names.

Felt Board Story

Picture for Abuelita

More than anything, Belinda ❶ liked to paint pictures. Today she was going to make a beautiful painting to give to her grandma, or *Abuelita. Abuelita* was coming to Puerto Rico to visit Belinda tomorrow.

On this beautiful morning, Belinda was carefully getting ready to paint the blue water around the island. She put paper, pencils, and brushes in her basket. ❷ She might get hungry so she packed an orange, a plum, a sandwich, and a bottle of juice. ❸ Last she put a tube of blue paint in her basket. ❹

Just a step before she leapt out the door, Belinda began some worrisome wondering. What if when she started to paint the water, she saw red and orange flowers growing nearby? To paint the flowers she would have to run home and get her red and orange paints. That would take some time. And then, she might not have enough time to finish the picture for her grandma. So Belinda went to her paint box, got out her red ❺ and orange tubes of paint, ❻ and placed them in the basket.

Just a step before she leapt out the door, Belinda began some worrisome wondering again. What if the sunshine made yellow shimmers on the water? To paint them she would have to go home, get her yellow paint, and hurry back. But then, would she have time to finish the picture for her grandma? So Belinda got her yellow paint, ❼ and added it to the basket.

Just a step before she leapt out the door, Belinda

began some more worrisome wondering. Would there be green leaves around the flowers growing near the water? If so, she would need green. So she dropped green ❽ into the basket.

Just a step before she leapt out the door, Belinda began some worrisome wondering. The day was getting cloudy. Would the shadows on the water be purple? She added her purple paint ❾ to the very full basket just in case. In her basket she now had red, orange, yellow, green, blue, and purple paints. With those colors she could paint almost anything.

Belinda stepped out the door and found out it had begun to rain. "Oh, no!" she said. "I won't need all those colors now. I will just need gray." So she added her gray ❿ paint to the basket but forgot to take out the other colors. She also took her umbrella. ⓫

As she sat down to paint, a beautiful rainbow spread across the sky. Now she was glad she had brought so many colors. To paint the rainbow, she used red, orange, yellow, green, blue, and purple. Belinda knew this was the best picture she had ever painted.⓬ Her *Abuelita* thought it was perfect. She had it framed and hung it in her house to remember her visit.

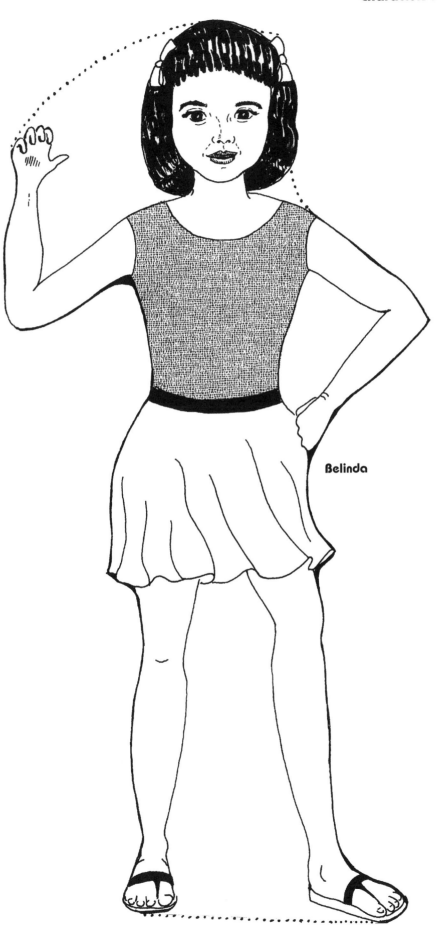

Belinda

Characters for Picture for Abuelita

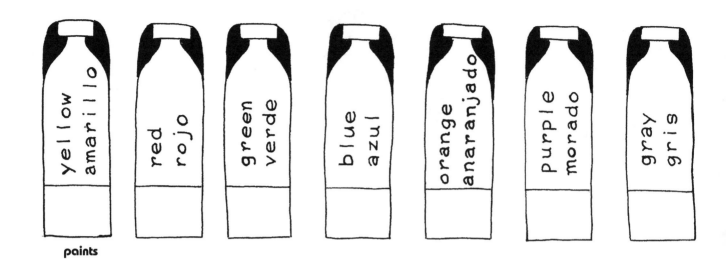

yellow amarillo
red rojo
green verde
blue azul
orange anaranjado
purple morado
gray gris

paints

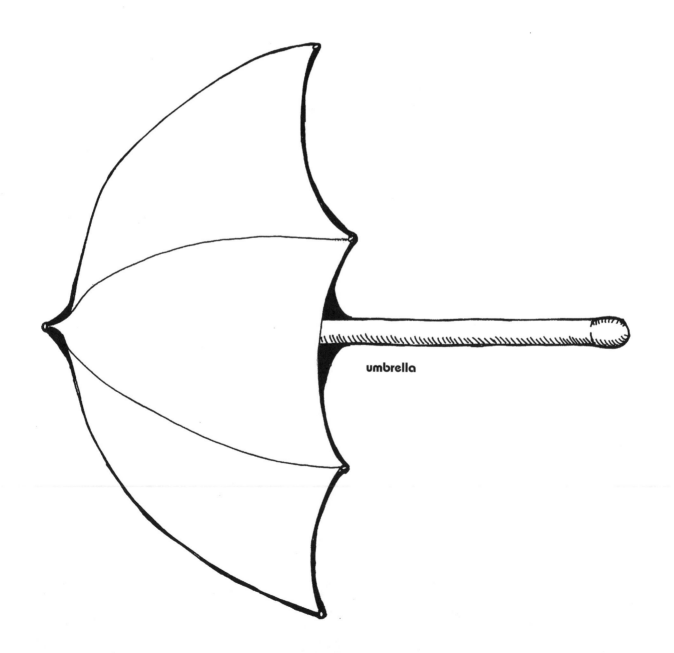

umbrella

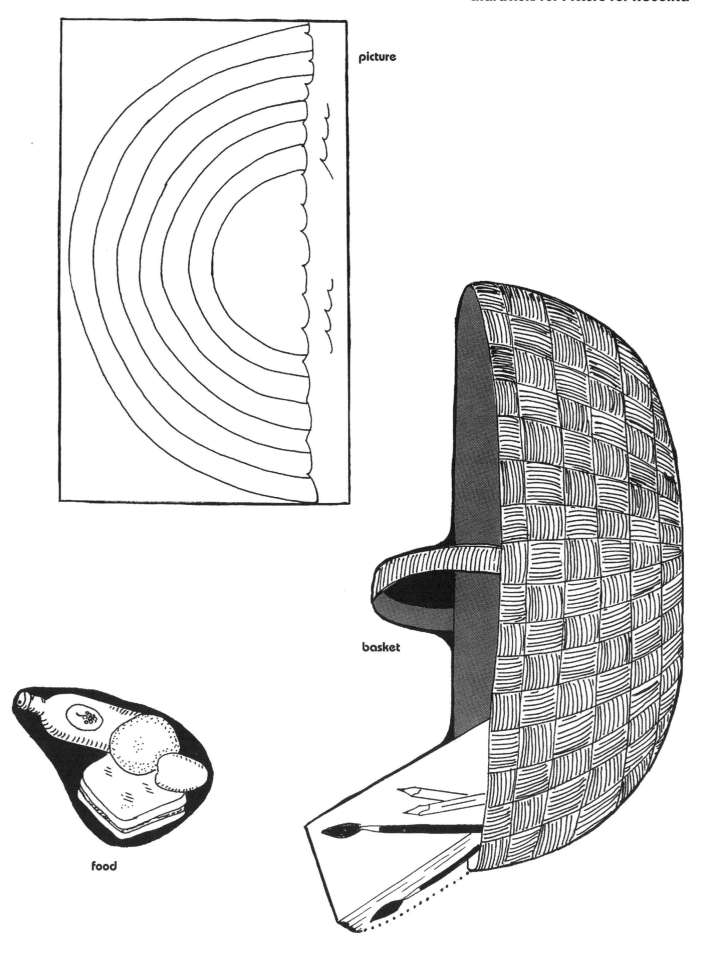

picture

basket

food

Hints for Coloring Felt Characters

Color the ends of the paint tubes to match the colors written on them. As you tell the story, point to the paint tubes and let the children name the colors as they are added to the basket. The rainbow's stripes in the picture are red, orange, yellow, green, blue, and purple. Otherwise, use your imagination as you choose colors.

Movements of Felt Characters

This story is simple to tell because each piece is added to the felt board and remains in place throughout the story. Before you begin, position the felt board vertically. Remember that all directions assume you are facing the front of the board.

❶ Place Belinda in the center of the board.

❷ Position her basket to the right of her, as if it were resting on the floor beside her.

❸ Add the food piece, placing it next to the paper, pencils, and brushes.

❹ Put the blue paint near the food. As you add the paints, pile them horizontally or vertically above the basket making sure that each flannel piece is fully on the board so it does not slip. It will make a very full basket, but this is part of the fun of the story.

❺ Fit the red paint into the basket.

❻ Add the orange paint to the basket.

❼ Add the yellow paint.

❽ Add the green paint.

❾ Add the purple paint.

❿ Place the gray paint above the basket.

⓫ Place the umbrella over Belinda's head with the handle just left of her upraised hand.

⓬ Put the picture to the right of her.

The story ends with all the pieces on the felt board. Belinda stands with the umbrella over her, the basket full of the paints and food in the lower right corner, and the picture in the upper right of the board.

Second Activity Using Characters

Missing Color

Ask the children to name the six primary and secondary colors: red, orange, yellow, green, blue, and purple. As they name a color, place the paint tube of that color on the felt board. When they are all there, it is time to begin the game Missing Color.

This is a memory game. For the simplest version place the six colors in spectrum order. Obscure the children's view by holding up a large piece of cardboard or asking them to close their eyes. Remove one color. Ask them to look again and guess what color is missing.

To make the game harder, place the colors in random order on the felt board in the beginning of each game. Play as before. The most difficult version is to remove the six color tubes and return five of them in a completely different order than they were previously.

Chant during each game as you are removing a color:

> I know the colors of the rainbow.
> Do you know them too?
> If one color were missing,
> I'd know the hue.
> Would you?"

Creative Activities

Art Activity:
Make an Arpillera (ar-pee-YAIR-ah)

Arpilleras are wall hangings put together from cut and sewn pieces of cloth. They were first made in Chile, South America, to show important events in day to day life. They are now made in other South American Countries like Peru, and Columbia.

Make an *arpillera* of flowers as a group project. Prepare a garden patch by cutting a piece of green burlap to 14 inches wide and about 20 inches long. Extend the length of the burlap for a group larger than twenty-five children. Overlap the width two inches on a metal hanger and secure with safety pins.

Cut an assortment of two or three-inch long petals from felt. Make a small slit near one end of each petal by folding the petal lengthwise and snipping. Let each child choose three to five petals of the same color. Have the children string the petals on a four-inch piece of green pipe cleaner. Next, push the petals together to form a flower. They can then fold down the top of the pipe cleaner two or three times to form the flower's center. Let the children plant their flower by weaving the stems into the burlap. Now you have made a garden-of-flowers *arpillera*.

Science Activity: Sorting

Bring three similar objects in the three, pigment primary colors, red, blue, and yellow. You might try candles, plastic forks, squares of paper, scarfs, blocks or any other objects that you can find in these colors. Let the children look at and feel the objects. Have the children sort the objects by color, then by object, then by hardness or softness, then by smoothness.

Color Game: Go Fish

Cut out fish shapes from construction paper using the eight rainbow colors. Attach a large paper clip to each. Make a fishing pole from a dowel with a string attached. At the end of the string, tie a magnet. Let the children fish. Talk about the color of each fish caught. If the number of children who are fishing is large, use two or more poles. While fishing, sing the tune "Farmer in the Dell." Use these words:

> A fishing we will go.
> A fishing we will go.
> Hi-ho-the derry-o.
> A fishing we will go.

Cassette source: *Early Early Childhood Songs* by Ella Jenkins. New York: Folkways, 1972. Music source: *Jane Yolen's Mother Goose Songbook.* Honesdale, Pa.: Boyds Mill, 1992.

Language Development: What is Red?

Start with one of the six primary and secondary colors: red, orange, yellow, green, blue, purple. Hold up a piece of paper or a crayon or you could use the felt pieces of the paint tubes. Ask the children to name things that are that color. Give them hints when they get stuck. Then go on to the next color until you have gone through all six colors. Some things can be many different colors, for example, grapes can be green or purple and T-shirts can be almost any color.

Resources for Story Time

Poems

"What is Pink?" by Christina G. Rossetti. From *Sing a Song of Popcorn*. New York: Scholastic, 1988.

Good illustrations.

Hailstones and Halibut Bones by Mary O'Neill. New York: Doubleday, 1961.

Poems about many colors.

Books

Rainbow of My Own by Don Freeman. New York: Viking, 1966.

A boy plays with a rainbow.

White Is the Moon by Valerie Greeley. New York: Macmillan, 1990.

A lyrical view of our natural world told through colors. Unfortunately, red as in a fox is not a true red, but the rhyme and illustrations make it noteworthy nevertheless.

The Princess and the Painter by Jane Johnson. New York: Farrar Strauss & Giroux 1994.

What might have happened to a Spanish princess when Velazquez painted *Las Meninas*.

Color Dance by Ann Jonas. New York: Greenwillow, 1989.

In this simple concept book dancers mix colors using veils of red, blue, yellow, black, grey, and white. Again, the red is not true red.

Red Day, Green Day by Edith Kunhardt. New York:Greenwillow, 1992.

Andrew brings an object to kindergarten that is a different color each day.

Matthew's Dream by Leo Lionni. New York:Knopf, 1991.

After he visits an art museum, a mouse becomes a painter.

The Great Blueness and Other Predicaments by Arnold Lobel. New York: Harper & Row, 1968.

A wizard makes pots of paints to color the world.

Growing Colors by Bruce McMillan. New York: Lothrop, 1988.

Photographs of fruits and vegetables in many colors. No story, but fun for participation and sharing.

Brown Bear, Brown Bear, What Do You See? by Bill Martin. New York: Holt, Rinehart, and Winston, 1967.

A simple, rhyming book about colors that invites participation.

Red Riding Hood by James Marshall. New York: Dial, 1987.

This familiar folktale told Marshall style is sure to delight.

The Little Painter of Sabana Grande by Patricia Markum. New York: Bradbury, 1993.

Fernando, a young artist in Panama, has no paper for his colorful paints, so he paints houses.

Mary Wore Her Red Dress by Merle Peek. New York: Clarion, 1985.

Texas folk song with the music included. After reading or singing the song, add verses that point out the colors of the clothing of the children in your group.

Mouse Paint by Ellen Stoll Walsh. San Diego: Harcourt, 1989.

A delightful mix of concepts and story using three mice, a cat, and three jars of paint.

Seven Blind Mice by Ed Young. New York: Philomel, 1992.

This adaption of a folktale from India called "The Blind Man and the Elephant" uses seven colorful mice.

Music

"Bein' Green." Cassette source: *A Sesame Street Celebration* by Jim Henson. New York: Sesame Street, 1991.

Kermit the frog explains that it is not easy being green.

"Rainbow Zoo." Cassette source: *Rainbow Zoo* by Partners in Song. Columbia, Md.: Partners in Song, 1993.

A short, fun song about colorful animals.

Video

"I Know the Colors in the Rainbow" from *Ella Jenkins for the Family*. Cambridge, Mass.: Smithsonian Folkways, 1991.

A music video.

9. It's a Wonderful World

Introduction

This chapter includes stories, songs, and poems about the beauty of the world. The story, "A Bend in the Stream" shows how one, small child made a difference. His gentle protests focused the neighbors' attention on a need to clean up a nearby stream. While you could use this theme anytime, the felt story makes it especially appropriate in the springtime when people clean up the outdoors.

The second activity with the felt characters is a cumulative story about a trip to the ice cream shop. This is also an event that often takes place in warmer weather. The story is called "Going to Get Ice Cream."

The activities and resources in this chapter show nature's variety: insects, rainforests, leaves, trees, ponds, rain, sun, and stars. Some materials encourage children to explore nature and marvel at the small and large wonders that surrounds them. Others point out everyone's duty to keep our world clean and to use its resources wisely.

Felt Board Story

The Bend in the Stream

After breakfast Ralph ❶ stopped at the bend in the stream ❷ behind their house. Bottles, ❸ cans, and squashed cups littered the banks. An old tire ❹ and smashed, cardboard boxes lay half buried inside the stream's curve. In the sludge sat ❺ car parts and a rusty wagon. The water was dark and still. He took a deep breath, wrinkled his nose, and said, "Phew!" Ralph was a shy boy of few words. He knew he could never clean up the stream by himself.

Everyone he had seen that morning was busy doing important things. His sister was practicing for the spring concert. His mother was grading papers. Doctor Chang was mowing his lawn. Mrs. Lowe stood high on a ladder washing her windows. So Ralph went home and waited. ❻

When his sister finished practicing, ❼ Ralph said, "Come," and led her down to the stream. ❽

"Yuck," his sister said. She threw her apple core into the stream. Ralph heard a *gaaaalug* as the core oozed it way into the muck.

"No," he said. He reached his hand into the cold, slimy water, but he could not find the core.

"Look! You are one kid. It would take the whole neighborhood to clean up this mess. I have homework to do," his sister said. ❾ After lunch Ralph led his mother ❿ to the bend in the stream. "Look," he said and pointed.

"How terrible," she said. "It would take a long pull, a strong pull, a pull all together to fix this place."

Ralph went to the edge of the stream, grabbed the rope tied to the tire, and tugged. "Oh, all right," she said. Side by side, they dragged the tire and some soggy boxes ⓫ out of the stream. "But we can not do this alone."

"Get help," Ralph said. And they did. Soon their next-door neighbors were helping. ⓬ With joined strength, the four hoisted out a car engine and a rusty wagon. ⓭ It was obvious that the four of them could never clean up this whole area alone.

"Get more help," Ralph said.

Soon, the whole street ⓮ was cleaning and improving the stream. Working shoulder to shoulder, they removed the cups, bottles, and cans from in and around the stream. ⓯ When the debris was gone, the water began to flow. Doctor Chang brought an old bench from his yard. Mr. Lowe painted it white, and Mrs. Lowe planted flowers around it. ⓰ Mother named it Little Bend Nook.

That evening everyone in the neighborhood had a picnic there. ⓱ They shared a bucket of fried chicken, potato salad, carrots, and watermelon. Ralph's sister asked, "How did you do it?" A brief, closed-mouth grin crossed Ralph's lips.

"Speech!" teased Mr. Lowe, who knew how shy Ralph was. But instead of hiding his head in his hands, Ralph, who had marshalled the neighborhood to clean up Little Bend Nook, stood up.

"Speech!" teased his sister. Ralph straightened the straps to his overalls. He climbed up on the bench. ⓲ They all got quiet. Ralph opened his mouth, cleared his throat, and said, "Hurrah!" Then he jumped down ⓳ to enjoy a popsicle by the bend in the stream.

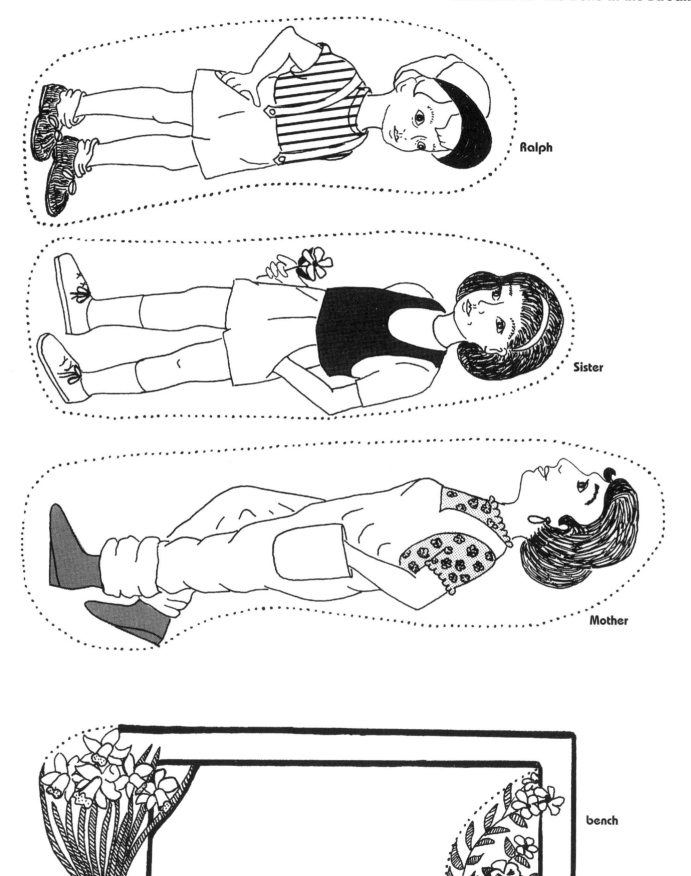

Ralph

Sister

Mother

bench

Characters for The Bend in the Stream

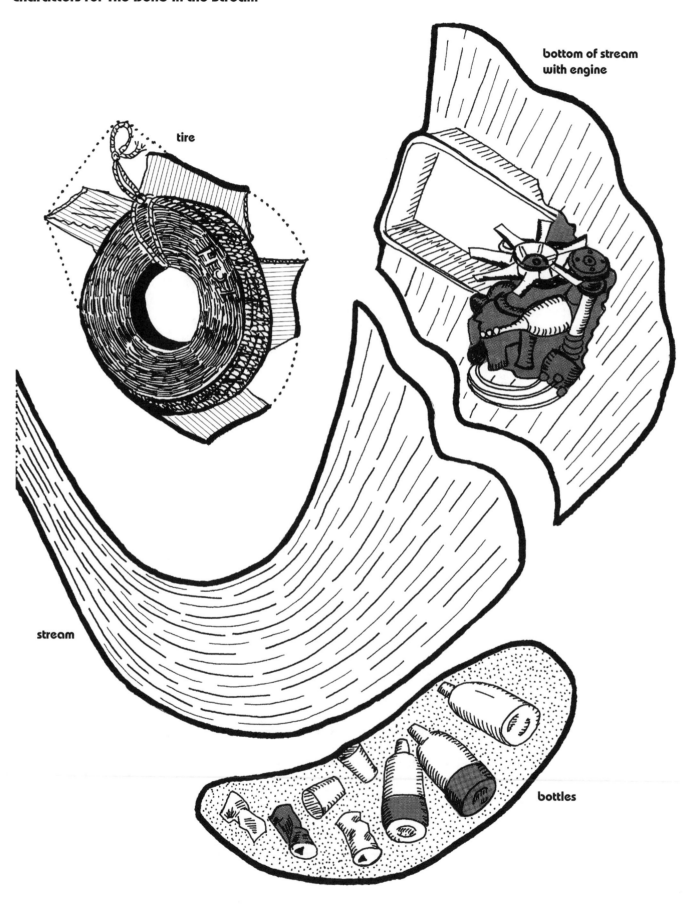

tire

bottom of stream with engine

stream

bottles

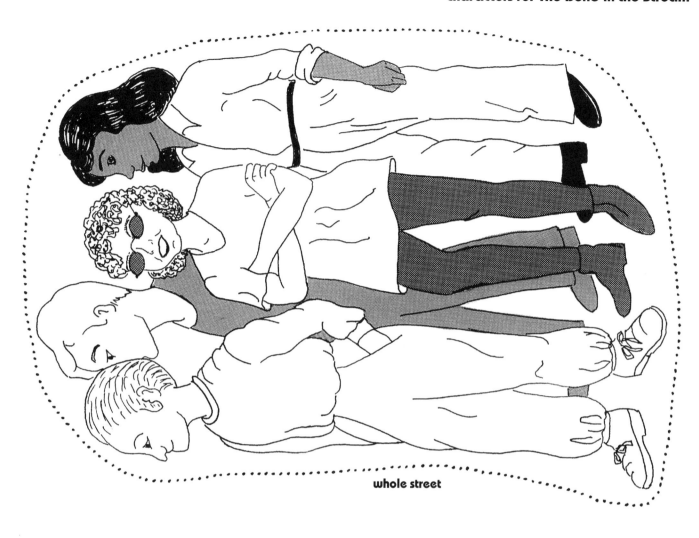

whole street

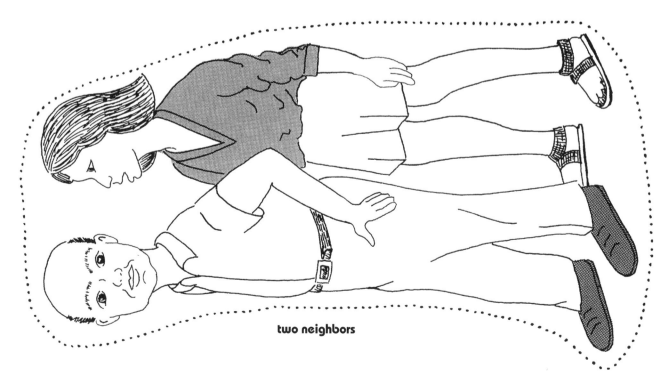

two neighbors

Movements of Felt Characters

The felt character's movements in this story are of medium complexity so you will need to practice them a few times before they are smooth. Begin with the long side of the board horizontal and the board empty. All left and right directions assume you are facing the front of the board.

❶ Place Ralph on the left side of the board.

❷ Add the stream in the lower left quarter of the board. Position the stream so it forms a C.

❸ Near the outside curve of the C, add the bottles and cups.

❹ Put the tire on the inside of the C so that the rope faces the right.

❺ Fit the lower portion of the stream that contains the car engine to the top part of the stream like a puzzle piece.

❻ Move Ralph to the upper left corner.

❼ Hold out the character of his sister so the children can identify her.

❽ Place Ralph and his sister to the right of the stream so they face each other.

❾ Remove Sister, but keep this character close because she will be used again. Leave Ralph on the board.

❿ Put Mother facing Ralph.

⓫ Take off the tire piece.

⓬ Add the two neighbors to the right of Mother.

⓭ Remove the piece with the engine in it.

⓮ Place the group of four to the right of the two neighbors.

⓯ Remove the piece with the cans, bottles, and cups on it.

⓰ Add the bench above the stream.

⓱ Position Sister to the right of the group.

⓲ Put Ralph above the bench, being sure not to overlap the pieces. It should look like he is standing on the bench.

⓳ Jump Ralph down from the bench and place him where he had been previously.

The story ends with the following pieces on the board from left to right: the stream with the bench above it, Ralph, Mother, two neighbors, the group from their street, and Sister.

Second Activity Using Characters

Going to Get Ice Cream

This is a short, cumulative story using the people from the felt story. **(Place Ralph in the left half of the board. Add his sister to face him.)**

"I'm going to get an ice cream cone," said Ralph's sister.

"To get to the ice cream shop, you'll have to walk past the haunted house, over the bridge, and around the cemetery," Ralph said. "Better not go alone."

His sister thought of cackling witches at a haunted house. "I'll go back and get Mom," she said. And she did. **(Move sister back to the right. Bring sister with mother behind her to face Ralph.)**

"We're going to get ice cream cones," said Ralph's sister and mother.

"To get to the ice cream shop, you'll have to walk past the haunted house, over the bridge, and around the cemetery," he said. "Better not go alone."

His sister thought of witches. His mother thought of trolls under a bridge. "We'll go back and get the neighbors," they said. And they did. **(Move sister and mother back to the right. Bring sister, mother, and neighbors to face Ralph.)**

"We're going to get ice cream cones," his sister, mother, and neighbors said.

"To get to the ice cream shop, you'll have to walk past the haunted house, over the bridge, and around the cemetery," he said. "Better not go alone."

His sister thought of witches. His mother thought of trolls. His neighbors thought of ghosts in the cemetery. "We'll go back and get some friends," they said. And they did. **(Move sister, mother, and neighbors back to the right. Bring sister, mother, neighbors, and group of four friends to face Ralph.)**

"We're going to get ice cream cones," said his sister, mother, neighbors, and friends.

"To get to the ice cream shop, you'll have to walk past the haunted house, over the bridge, and around the cemetery," he said. "Better not go alone."

His sister thought of witches. His mother thought of trolls. His neighbors thought of ghosts in the cemetery. But their friends asked, "Why? Are there witches, trolls, or ghosts ahead?"

"Oh, no," said Ralph. "But you had better not go without me. I know the way."

Creative Activities

Science Activity: Nature Walk

Take a nature walk in a nearby park or woods. Let the children collect bits of nature that have fallen on the ground. Then sort the object into piles such as leaves, acorns and other seeds, pine cones, rocks, and twigs.

Science Activity: Feel Bag

Put an object found on your walk in a bag. Without letting the children look, have them put their hand in the bag and feel the object. Let them guess what it is. Repeat with other natural objects.

Cherry Stone Game: Native American Game

This is a simplified version of a Native American game of luck. Take six cherry or plum pits and paint one side of each white and the other black. Children take turns shaking the stones in a large bowl. When they set the bowl down, let them count the number of pits with the black side face-up. This is their score. You may prefer not to tally the points or have a winner. Either way the children will enjoy the game just to see how many stones turn up black.

Language Development: Talk in Five Languages

Teach your children to say world in five languages: world (WUHRLD) in English, *mondo* (MON-doh) in Italian, *monde* (MOHN-d) in French, *mundo* (MOON-doh) in Spanish. Several Plains Indian tribes such as Blackfeet, Crow, Sioux, Cheyenne, Arapaho, and Kiowa developed a sign language to speak with each other. They signed earth by pointing down with their right index finger. Then, they reach down to the ground and rub their thumb against the tips of their first two fingers of their right hand.

Resources for Story Time

Poems

"Dragonfly," "Beetles," and "The Walking Stick." From *Demi's Secret Garden* compiled by Demi. New York: Holt, 1993.

   Fabulously illustrated by Demi.

"Lady Bug, Lady Bug." From *Chinese Mother Goose Rhymes* edited by Robert Wyndham. Cleveland: World Publishing, 1968.

A Chinese Mother Goose poem nicely illustrated by Ed Young with Chinese writing on the side.

Little Robin Redbreast: A Mother Goose Rhyme. New York: North-South, 1994.

This picture book version of the nursery rhyme is illustrated by Shari Halpern.

Out and About by Shirley Hughes. New York: Lothrop, 1988.

Many short poems colorfully illustrated about the wonders of nature. Good for sharing a few at a time.

"Daffy-down-dilly," and "Mary, Mary, Quite Contrary." From *The Random House Book of Mother Goose.* New York: Random House, 1986.

Traditional nursery rhymes.

Books

Where Does the Trail Lead? by Burton Albert. New York: Simon & Schuster, 1991.

A young, African American boy wanders on Summertime Island through buttercups, cattails, and along the shore until he returns to his family.

Trees by Harry Behn. New York: Holt, 1992.

A short poem about the importance of trees. Beautifully illustrated by James Endicott.

Golden Egg Book by Margaret Wise Brown. Racine, Wis.: Western, 1947.

A bunny wonders what is inside an egg in this simple story of friendship.

Very Hungry Caterpillar by Eric Carle. New York: Philomel, 1983.

The little caterpillar eats his way through various foods, forms a cocoon, and becomes a butterfly. A favorite.

Wild Wild Sunflower Child Anna by Nancy Carlstrom. New York: Macmillan, 1987.

A celebration of Anna, a black girl who revels in the beauty of nature. Wonderfully illustrated by Jerry Pinkney.

Legend of the Bluebonnet, retold by Tomie dePaola. New York: Putnam, 1983.

Beautiful but sad legend of a Cherokee girl who gives up her most precious possession for her tribe. Too sad for use with preschoolers.

Red Leaf, Yellow Leaf by Lois Ehlert. San Diego: Harcourt, 1991.

Colorful graphics accompany a child's description of the growth of her maple tree. Useful in autumn too because it shows colorful fall leaves.

In Tthe Small, Small Pond by Denise Fleming. New York: Holt, 1993.

From spring to autumn, the small pond teems with activity. Simple, short and bright.

3 Pandas Planting by Megan Halsey. New York: Macmillan, 1994.

While counting down from twelve, this books shows ways to take care of the earth. A good introduction to a discussion.

Is This a House for a Hermit Crab? by Megan McDonald. Orchard, 1990.

A crab tries many places before he finds the right house, just in time. Simple and repetitive, with nice pastel drawings.

The Salamander Room by Anne Mazer. New York: Knopf, 1991.

Brian imagines changing his room until it is a perfect home for the salamander he finds in the woods.

April Showers by George Shannon. New York: Greenwillow, 1995.

Frogs joyously dance in the rain in this rollicking, rhythmic celebration.

House of Leaves by Kiyoshi Soya. New York: Philomel, 1986.

A Japanese girl finds a house of leaves to protect her from the rain. Then, she lets insects share her shelter.

Welcome to the Green House by Jane Yolen. New York: Putnam, 1993.

A poetic introduction to the tropical rainforest and its animals. Beautiful illustrations by Laura Regan.

Music

"This Land is Your Land." Cassette source: *We Are America's Children* by Ella Jenkins. Washington, D.C.: Smithsonian Folkway Records, 1989.

A celebration of the natural beauty of the United States.

"One Light, One Sun." Cassette source: *Evergreen, Everblue* by Raffi. Willowdale, Ont.: Shoreline, 1990.

A song about the sun lighting all the world's people.

"Garden Song." Cassette source: *Let's Clean Up Our Act: Songs for the Earth* by Tom Callinan and Ann Shapiro. Guilford, Conn.: American Melody, 1989.

Rhythmic song to play while planting seeds.

"Twinkle, Twinkle, Little Star." Cassette source: *Hap Palmer Sings Classic Nursery Rhymes.* Feeport, N.Y.:Educational Activities, 1991. Music source: *Go in and out the Window* edited by Dan Fox. New York: Metropolitan Museum of Art, 1987.

Video

The Lorax. New York: Columbia Broadcasting System, 1972.

Animated version of Dr. Seuss's story about the Lorax who tries to save the forest from the Once-ler, who is only interested in cutting down the trees for profit. 30 min.

10. Celebrate Me

Introduction

Every child is special and should be proud to be unique. This chapter focuses on self-esteem, self-confidence, and taking care of oneself.

The felt board story, "Just Plain Horace," is about a cat who is not happy with himself. He finds a magic sea shell and wishes for things he thinks will make him better. Later he realizes he is happy being just plain Horace.

The second activity is a countdown poem reusing the five cats from the felt board story. Use this activity after "Just Plain Horace" otherwise references to the characters and events will be confusing.

The creative activities include a discussion of each child's special qualities which will bolster the children's self-esteem. Three activities encourage good health habits: Learning the Five Food Groups, Talk about Sharing, and Wiggle Your Body Parts. The resources include stories, poems, and videos that show unique individuals who are or become happy with themselves. A couple of stories and music selections deal with emotions. One picture book makes learning safety tips fun.

Felt Board Story

Just Plain Horace

Nobody noticed Horace all morning. When Winthrop ❶ walked by, Horace said, "Let's go to the beach and play Super Cats."

"Can't," his friend said. "I need to practice my trumpet. I have a recital tomorrow". ❷

So Horace wandered alone and unnoticed toward the beach. He jumped up and touched a petal on one of the dogwood trees that lined the road. No one noticed how high he jumped. No one noticed how brave he was to dip a paw into the cold water at the shore. He stared at his image in the water. "No wonder nobody notices me," he said aloud. "I am just plain Horace. Oh, I wish, I wish, I wish…"

He was surprised when a striped shell ❸ near him said, "I can make all your wishes come true 'cause I'm a magic shell with nothin' better to do."

Horace picked up the shell, "Make me blue."

"And?"

"Give me wings."

"And?"

"A dragon's tail." Faster than he could say, "Super Cat," he was blue with wings and had a dragon's tail. ❹ Grinning at the shell, he wished for a long horn, ❺ curly hair, ❻ and a fan of feathers on his feet. ❼ When he saw his reflection, he said, "I'm a Super Cat!"

"Let's show off my new look," he said. So off to the playground he strutted, as well as he could strut with a huge tail. He tried to jump at the dogwood tree but his wings got in the way. He heard screaming and scurrying ahead, but when he got to the park, it was empty.

He headed home to surprise Mom and Pop. ❽ "See your Super Cat," he said, but instead of *ooing* and *ahing* his parents backed away and looked frightened. "I'm your Horace," he said.

"You sound like our Horace, but you are not our Horace. You are blue with wings and a dragon's tail. You have a horn, curly hair, and feathered feet. Our Horace is special. Now shoo!" They herded Horace outside and slammed the door. ❾

His fan of feathered feet began to tickle. His eyes burned. "Magic shell, make me just plain Horace again," he said.

"Not so easy," said the magic shell. "How about a long white beard with ribbons in it?" Horace shook his head. "Fangs?" Again, Horace shook his head. "Polka dots?"

"No! I want to be just plain Horace. I want to go home."

"Then you must find me someone else to be my master. Then I can cancel your wishes."

Horace thought. He listened to Winthrop's sweet, trumpet music drifting from next door. "Winthrop?"

"Might as well try. I sure like his music," said the shell.

"He practices a lot." Horace tiptoed next door and tap, tap, tapped ❿ on the window. "Winthrop, do you want some wishes?"

"Sure, but not until after my recital," said Winthrop.

The shell agreed and Winthrop came outside to get the magic shell. ⓫

"Wow," Winthrop said when he saw Horace. "You had imaginative wishes." When Winthrop picked up the shell, ⓬ Horace changed.

First the fan of feathered feet, ⓭ the curly hair, ⓮ and then the single horn disappeared. ⓯ Then faster than he could say "Super Cat," the wings and tail were gone and he was no longer blue. ⓰ He was just plain Horace again. ⓱

He raced home. ⓲ His Mom and Pop ran out to greet him, ⓳ pet him, and tell him how much they love him. They went inside to hear Pop's story of the strange cat who pretended to be their Horace. ⓴

After Winthrop had a perfect recital, he disappeared. ㉑ For three days Horace ㉒ grinned at stories he heard about a trumpet playing cat on a magic carpet.

Just when Horace missed him the most, Winthrop returned. ㉓ Winthrop said, "It was fun, but I'm glad to be me."

"Me too," said Horace.

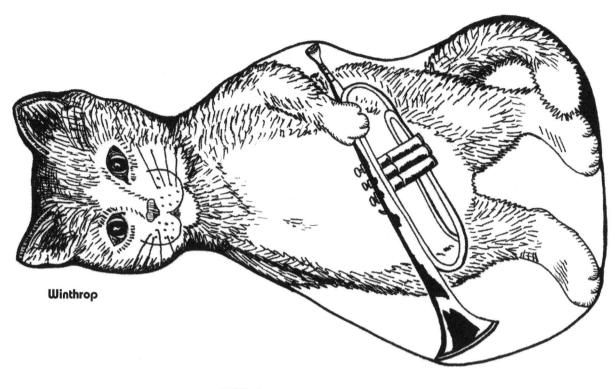

Winthrop

magic shell

Horace

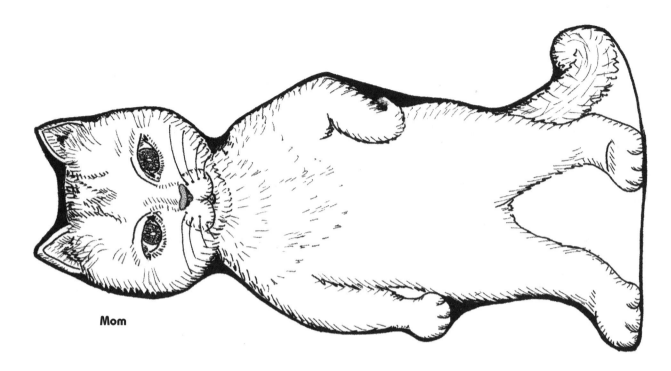

Mom

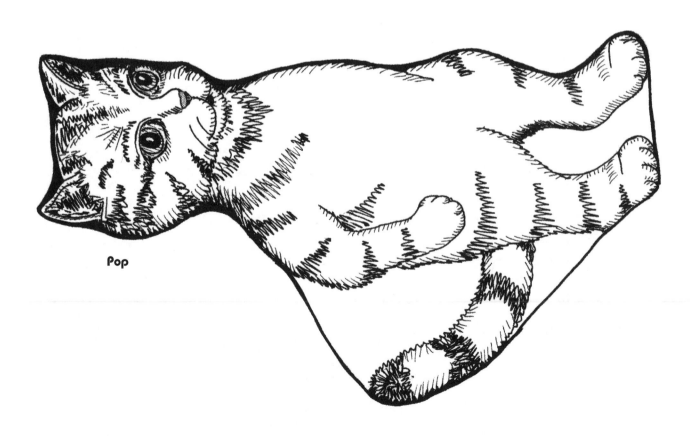

Pop

Characters for Just Plain Horace

horn

hair

hair

blue Horace

feathers

Hints for Making Felt Characters

The felt characters for this story are not as easy to cut out as those in other stories. The magic additions, the horn, the hair, and the fan of feathered feet, need to fit closely to Horace, similar to their positions on the page of felt characters. Cut the characters on the thicker, outer lines. Be sure to keep the felt around the blue Horace and magic additions trimmed short. If you follow these precautions, the pieces will fit together better and the story will be more effective.

Color Horace and Winthrop dull colors like light gray or tan. The blue Horace should be bright blue. The wings, tail, horn, hair, and feathers should be bright colors so that when Horace is finished with his wishes, he looks wild.

Movements of Felt Characters

Begin the story with the long side of the felt board horizontal and Horace in its center. All left and right directions assume you are facing the board.

❶ Put Winthrop to the right of Horace as if the two are walking together.

❷ Take Winthrop off the board. You will need this piece later.

❸ Place the magic shell left of Horace.

❹ Remove Horace and replace him with the blue Horace. The shell remains near the blue Horace.

❺ Add the horn on top of Horace's head .

❻ Place a curly hairpiece on each side of Horace's head, between his horn and wings.

❼ Put the feathers just below his feet.

❽ Add Mom and Pop to the left and slightly above Horace.

❾ Remove Mom and Pop.

❿ Tap three times on something hard, like a table.

⓫ Place Winthrop to the right and slightly below Horace.

⓬ Move the shell to the left side of Winthrop.

⓭ Remove the feathered feet.

⓮ Remove the curly hair.

⓯ Remove the horn.

⓰ Take the blue Horace off the board.

⓱ Place Horace on the board.

⓲ Pick up Horace and move him left and up.

⓳ Add Mom and Pop to the left of Horace.

⓴ Remove Mom, Pop, and Horace. Winthrop remains on the board with the shell.

㉑ Slip Winthrop and the shell from the board. The board is now empty.

㉒ Put Horace in the center of the board.

㉓ Place Winthrop to the right of him.

The story ends with Horace and Winthrop next to each other near the center of the board.

Second Activity Using Characters

Cat Countdown

Place the five cats on the felt board and recite this rhyme.

> Five little cats,
> Standing near a door,
> The wild one went inside,
> **(remove blue Horace)**
> Then there were **(pause to let the children fill in the number)** four.

> Four little cats,
> One climbed a tree, **(remove Mom)**
> Horace looked 'round and counted,
> And found there were **(pause)** three.

> Three little cats,
> With nothing left to do,
> One wished himself away, **(remove Pop)**
> And then there were **(pause)** two.

> Two little cats,
> Having lots of fun,
> Winthrop went to practice,
> **(remove Winthrop)**
> And that left **(pause)** one.

> Just Plain Horace,
> Still wanted to be a hero,
> So he chased after his dream,
> **(remove Horace)**
> And then there were **(pause)** zero.

Creative Activities

Language Activity: Talk about Being Special.

After the story, talk with the children about why Horace and Winthrop are special. Before he finds the magic shell, Horace is remarkable because he has a good imagination. He is a good friend. He can jump high. His parents love him. Then talk about what is special about his friend, Winthrop. He is musically talented, works hard, and is a good friend. He is also responsible because he chooses to finish the recital before having fun.

This discussion will help the children realize why they are special. Ask each child to name one thing about him or herself that is special. Children often do not realize why they are exceptional because their qualities are not flashy like being a movie star or a basketball hero. Let them know that friendliness, sweetness, and a sense of humor are valuable qualities.

Science Activity: Learn the Five Food Groups

Learning about nutrition will help children take good care of themselves. Find a picture of the food pyramid. Talk with the children about the foods in each group. Cut pictures of foods from magazines and talk about what category they fit into. Put together meals from the pictures and see how many groups are in each meal. An excellent resource for this activity with a picture of the food pyramid is *The Edible Pyramid: Good Eating Every Day* by Loreen Leedy. New York: Holiday, 1994.

Language Activity: Talk About Sharing.

Talk about the things people share such as toys, playground equipment, teachers, and library books. Then talk about the things we should not share such as toothbrushes, hair brushes, washcloths, drinking cups, combs, spoons, forks, and handkerchiefs. Both sharing and not sharing are healthy ways to take care of ourselves.

Active Song: Wiggle Your Body Parts

Tell the children that exercise is another way to take care of themselves. Change the words to the tune, "If You're Happy and You Know It." Use these new words:

> If I'm happy and I know it, I'll wiggle my head.
>
> If I'm happy and I know it, I'll wiggle my head.
>
> If I'm happy and I know it, I'll exercise and show it.
>
> If I'm happy and I know it, I'll wiggle my head.

Use leg, arm, hands, fingers, hand, and foot for the next six verses. If the children are still interested, continue the song using body parts that are difficult to wiggle such as chin, hair, ear, nose, elbow, and knee. For these verses substitute "point to my..." for "wiggle my...." The music source is listed in the resource section.

Japanese Game: Fukuwarai

Japanese children play this game during their New Year's celebration, but children enjoy it anytime. This adaption of the game is similar to Pin the Tail on the Donkey. Draw the outline of a face on a large piece of paper and tape it to a wall. From construction paper cut facial features such as eyes, a nose, a mouth, eyebrows, ears, and hair to fit the face. Give each child a facial feature with a circle of tape on the back. Blindfold one child at a time and aim him or her at the wall toward the outline of a face. Help the blindfolded child extend his or her arm so that the tape on the facial feature will stick to the paper. Enjoy the funny face you make. Repeat this game as often as you wish until all children have participated.

Resources for Story Time

Poems

"Cherish Me" by Joyce Carol Thomas. From *Brown Honey in Broomwheat Tea.* New York: HarperCollins, 1993.

> Beautiful illustration.

"You-Tu" by Charlotte Pomerantz. From *The Tamarindo Puppy and Other Poems.* New York: Greenwillow, 1980.

> In English and Spanish. Good illustrations.

"Me I Am!" by Jack Prelutsky. From *The Random House Book of Poetry For Children.* New York: Random, 1983.

> A celebration of one's uniqueness with a full-page, black and white illustration.

Books

Otto Is Different by Franz Brandenberg. New York: Greenwillow, 1985.

> An octopus learns to appreciate having eight arms instead of two.

Mixed-up Chameleon by Eric Carle. New York: Crowell, 1984.

> A chameleon wishes to be like everybody in the zoo, and his wish comes true. Simple and colorful.

So What? by Miriam Cohen. New York: Greenwillow, 1982.

> Jim, a first grader, learns to accept himself. A gentle lesson.

Mean Soup by Betsy Everitt. San Diego: Harcourt, 1992.

> Horace copes with a bad day by making mean soup.

Chrysanthemum by Kevin Henkes. New York: Greenwillow, 1991.

> A little mouse learns that her unusual name really is perfect.

A Proper Little Lady by Nette Hilton. New York: Orchard, 1989.

Annabella dresses like a lady but underneath she is still Annabella.

Amazing Grace by Mary Hoffman. New York: Dial, 1991.

An exhilarating story about Grace, a young African American, who proves she can be anything she wants to be.

Leo the Late Bloomer by Robert Kraus. New York: Windmill, 1971.

His mother knew Leo would bloom if they just waited.

Silent Lotus by Jeanne M. Lee. New York: Farrar, Straus & Giroux, 1991.

A lovely, Vietnamese girl who cannot hear or speak learns her talent is dancing.

Tikki Tikki Tembo, retold by Arlene Mosel. New York: Holt, 1968.

The folktale of why Chinese parents give their children short names.

Bein' with You This Way by W. Nikola-Lisa. New York: Lee & Low, 1994.

In the park a little girl gathers her friends and enumerates their physical differences. Then she concludes they are all the same.

The Greatest Show on Earth by John Prater. Cambridge, Mass.: Candlewick, 1995.

Harry feels useless because everyone else in his family is a great circus performer. Then he finds his talent.

Officer Buckle and Gloria by Peggy Rathmann. New York: Putnam, 1995.

Officer Buckle and his police dog, Gloria, are popular visitors at schools with their safety program. A hilarious way to introduce safety tips.

Shy Charles by Rosemary Wells. New York: Dial, 1988.

Charles who is a shy, timid, and quiet mouse, rescues his babysitter in an emergency. Afterward, he remains shy, timid, and quiet.

Umbrella by Taro Yashima. New York: Viking, 1958.

Momo, a young Japanese American, cannot wait to use her new umbrella.

Music

"Head, Shoulders, Knees, and Toes." Cassette source: *Wee Sing* by Pamela Beall and Susan Nipp. Los Angeles: Price Stern Sloan, 1981. Music source: *Do Your Ears Hang Low?* edited by Tom Glazer. Garden City, New York: Doubleday, 1980.

"If You're Happy." Source cassette, *Good Morning Sunshine* by Patti Dallas and Laura Baron. Yellow Springs, Ohio: Golden Glow, 1985. Music source: *Do Your Ears Hang Low?* edited by Tom Glazer, Garden City, New York: Doubleday, 1980.

Video

"One of a Kind." From *Music and Magic*. Westlake, Calif.: Bright Ideas Productions, 1993.

A four-minute, musical segment with the positive message, "You're one of a kind and special to me."

"Potential." From *Music and Magic*. Westlake, Calif.: Bright Ideas Productions, 1993.

A rap music segment with the message, "You've got potential," for kids five and up.

11. Families

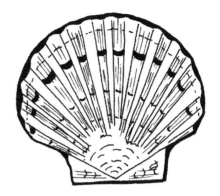

Introduction

This chapter focuses on families, a primary influence in children's lives. Families come in many sizes and have a wide variety of members, biologically related and not. In these stories about families, relatives, and ancestors, children recognize situations similar to their own and ones that are different.

The felt board story, "Watch out for Giant Toes!" is about two families. The first family is Derek and his father. During their summer vacation, Derek gets sick. His father entertains him with a tale about the second family, a family of mole crabs. Since the story within the story takes place at the beach in summer, it is most appropriate to use it during warm months.

The second activity with the felt characters is a song "Mole Crabs in the Sand," sung to the tune "The Wheels on the Bus." It is lively and participatory.

The resources in this chapter concentrate on positive relationships within families. Families of different ethnic backgrounds and various composition are shown to be loving and natural. Some stories involve parents and children; others are about brothers and sisters. There are a few tales about sibling rivalry and other minor troubles.

Felt Board Story

Watch Out for Giant Toes!

Derek lay in bed. His nose was runny; his eyes itched. His fever was 101. "I want to go to the beach," he said.

"We can't, son. You are too sick." He wiped Derek's forehead with a damp washcloth. "I'll cancel our first week's reservations. Maybe we can go next week."

"But..." Derek was too weak to protest further.

"Remember last year at the beach?" Dad asked softly. ❶ "Remember the soft, warm sand sloping down to the sea and the holes in the sand as the waves ❷ retreated?" Derek nodded and closed his eyes. "Busy, little mole crabs ❸ make those holes by digging tailfirst into the wet sand. Over and over again, they climb out, look around, and dig back into their burrows. ❹ Another one peeks out with his little black eyes at the ends of his antennae ❺ then digs in again."

"What are they looking for?" Derek asked.

"Danger, like seagulls wanting a crab dinner, or giant toes!" Dad tweaked Derek's toes through the blanket.

"Giant toes?"

"Sure. Mole crabs are less than two inches long, smaller than my thumb. Giant toes and mammoth feet could crush them. Well, one day, a mole crab named..."

"Molly". ❻

"Molly, it is. Well, Molly is surfing up and down the beach with her family, riding the waves then digging tailfirst into the sand, ❼ riding then digging, ❽ riding and digging. ❾ This is a backward family, like all mole crabs. They swim, crawl, and dig backward." Derek's father moved his hand backward over the bed-cover waves and burrowed it deep into the sheet of sand. Derek saw only Dad's two wiggling fingers stuck up in a V, like a mole crab's antenna. ❿

Derek asked, "How big is her family?"

"Let's say four. Nobody knows how they are related, but since they stick together and care for each other, they are a family."

"Like us," Derek said and gave Dad's hand a weak pat.

"Here comes another wave, right at Molly and her family. As it retreats, ⓫ one, two, three crabs emerge from the soaked sand, skitter toward the water, and burrow into the sand. All except Molly ⓬ who is blithely waving her feathery antennae catching plankton as fast as she can. Before she transfers the food to her mouth, the churned-up water spins her. She is confused and dizzy. A strong wave flicks her into the air. She lands up the beach on the hot, dry sand. ⓭

"Quickly, she digs, but the dry sand shifts around her. ⓮ Her eyes search for other familiar antennae sticking out of the sand, but she sees no one.

"She waits for the next wave, but it never reaches her. Molly scuttles toward the sea. ⓯ When she scurries around a scallop's shell, ⓰ she sees a swooping gull. ⓱ As fast as her legs can crawl, she backs under a piece of driftwood andigs. ⓲

The mole crab watches the mighty gull dive, swoop, then circle, looking for the tasty morsel it saw a moment ago. Then it veers off toward a family having a picnic. ⓳

"Molly has one leg out of the hole when down the beach comes giant toes. ⓴ There must be ten of them!"

"Look out for the giant toes, Molly," Derek called.

"Down the beach they come, *tha-bump, squish,* ㉑ *tha-bump, squish.* ㉒ Ten giant toes on the loose! *Tha-bump, squish.* Molly digs until the giant toes are right above her. Suddenly, a sand avalanche pours into her burrow and clogs the opening. *Tha-bump, squish, tha-bump, squish.* ㉓ Molly wiggles and digs upward with all eight legs on her egg-shaped body. With super-crab effort she stretches her breathing antennae into the air and climbs into the sunshine. ㉔

"She looks out over the vast sand. Beyond the remains of a sandcastle ㉕ is the shimmering sea. *Scritch-scratch.* ㉖ The sand is wetter and cooler here. With a slow *scritch-scratch* she rounds the castle's moat. She goes backward not looking where she is going but watching where she has been.

"A cool wave washes over her. When the *whoosh* of the wave subsides, Molly finds herself ㉗ in the midst of her waiting family. She is happy to be safe with them again."

"Better watch out Molly," Derek said. "I'm getting better and next week my family, twenty toes worth, will be running up and down the waves. So watch out for our giant toes!"

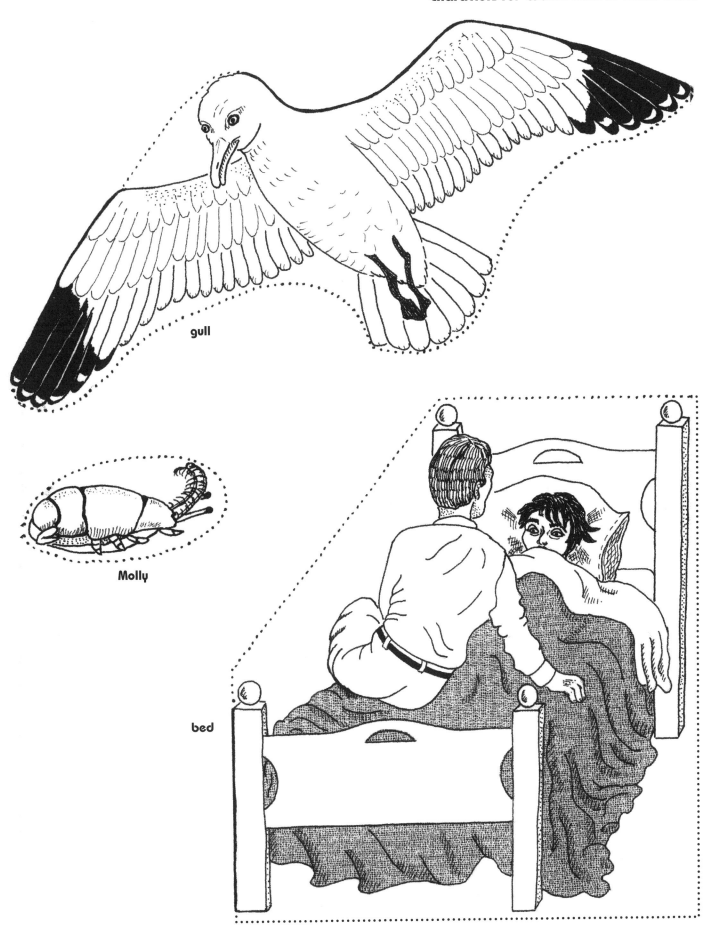

gull

Molly

bed

Characters for Watch Out for Giant Toes!

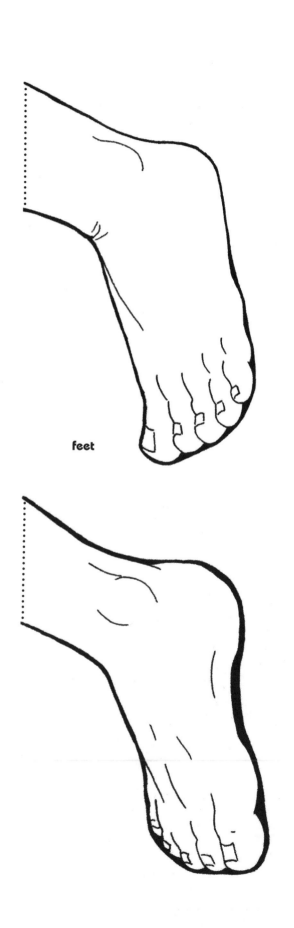

feet

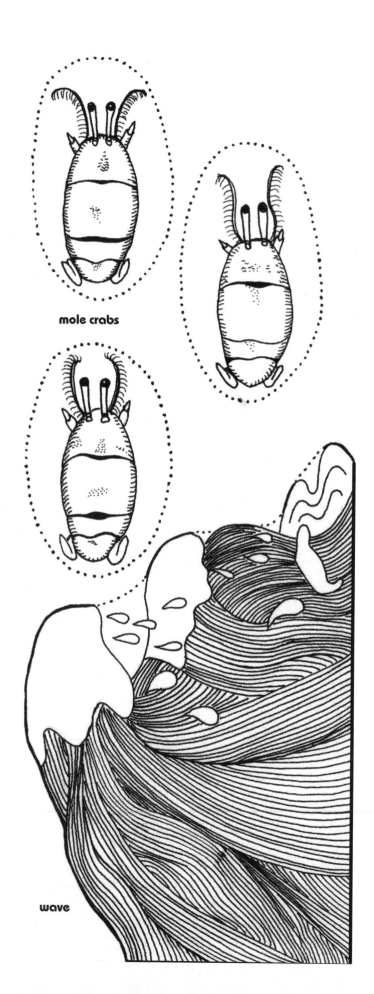

mole crabs

wave

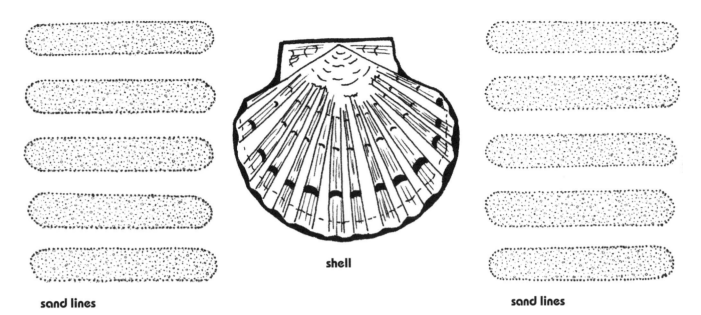

shell

sand lines

sand lines

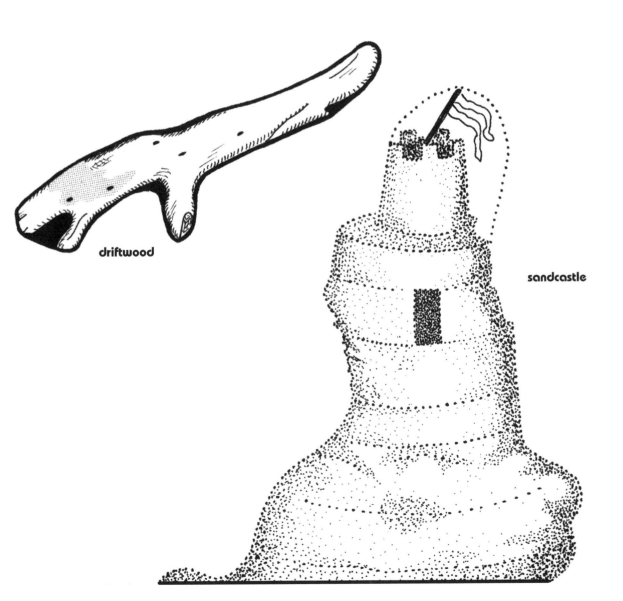

driftwood

sandcastle

Hints for Making Felt Characters

Color the crabs tan or gray and the sand lines tan. The number of sand lines you use will depend of the size of your felt board. My board is 3' long by 2' high and I use six lines. Longer boards will use more, shorter less.

Movements of Felt Characters

Position the felt board horizontally. All directions assume you are facing the front of the felt board. Begin the story with the bed in the upper, left-hand corner, where it remains throughout the story.

❶ Starting here and continuing through the next sentence, place the sand lines so they make a diagonal, dashed line from three inches below the top-right corner almost to the bottom-left corner. Leave space in the bottom-left corner for the wave. Allow a two-inch space between sand lines for the crabs to burrow in.

❷ Put the wave in the lower-left corner of the felt board. The sand and the wave will stay on the board until the story ends.

❸ Take one top-view crab and hold it over the space between the wave and the first sand line. Then scoot it backward below the sand line or into its burrow.

❹ Move another crab into the next available burrow.

❺ Place the last crab into the third hole. Three crabs are now burrowed between sand lines near the wave.

❻ Add Molly (the side-view crab) above the next space between sand lines.

❼ Dig her tail-first into her burrow.

❽ Slide Molly up and out of the burrow, then dig her back down.

❾ Repeat the previous action.

❿ As you say this sentence, hold up two fingers and wiggle them like antennae.

⓫ When you count the three crabs (all except Molly), move them above the sand line, then off the board to the left. You will need these three felt pieces later.

⓬ Move Molly above her burrow.

⓭ Put Molly to the far right above the sand line.

⓮ To pretend Molly digs, scoot her backward below the sand line.

⓯ Take Molly above the sand line and move her slightly left. Remember that she moves backward.

⓰ Add the scallop's shell above the sand line and move Molly around it.

⓱ Position the gull in the upper, right corner.

⓲ Add the driftwood just above Molly.

⓳ Fly the bird off to the left and take the shell and the driftwood off too. You will not need these pieces again.

⓴ Add the feet (above the sand) to the upper right side of the board.

㉑ Move one foot left.

㉒ Place the other foot to the left of the first foot, as if they were walking. The second foot should come down on top of Molly.

㉓ During "*tha-bump, squish, tha-bump, squish,*" walk the feet off the board to the left between the bed and the wave. You will not need the feet again.

㉔ Move Molly up so her antennae reach above the sand and place her above the sand line.

㉕ Put the sandcastle between Molly and the wave.

㉖ Move Molly to the left, around the sand-castle, and place her near the wave.

㉗ Position the three other crabs around Molly. The story ends with four crabs, the wave, the sand lines, the sandcastle, and the bed on the board.

Second Activity Using Characters

Mole Crabs in the Sand

Sing the following words to the tune "The Wheels on the Bus."

> Mole crabs in the sand go, dig, dig, dig.
> Dig, dig, dig; dig, dig, dig.
> Mole crabs in the sand go, dig, dig, dig,
> All at the beach.
>
> (During this verse place a mole crab on the board between sand lines. Move it below the sand lines during dig, dig, dig.)

Continue the song using the following verses and acting out what happens.

> Antennae on the crabs go, back and forth
> …All at the beach.
>
> Waves from the sea go, *whoosh, slap, shush*
> …All at the beach.
>
> (Put the wave on the board for this verse.)
>
> Gulls in the air go, *flap, flap, flap*
> …All at the beach.
>
> (Add the gull to the board for this verse.)
>
> Toes on the sand go, *tha-bump, squish*
> …All at the beach.
>
> (Walk feet across board during this verse.)

Continue the song by having the children make up verses about the beach.

Cassette source: *Rise And Shine* by Raffi. Willowdale, Ont.: Shoreline, 1982.

Music source: *2nd Raffi Songbook* by Raffi. New York: Crown, 1986.

Creative Activities

Listening Game: What Do I Hear?

Ask the children to listen. What sounds do they hear? Cars on the street? Birds? Gather several objects that can make noise like a whistle, bell, alarm clock, horn, egg beater, large paperback book. Let the children listen to the sounds the objects make. Flipping the pages of a book sounds different from turning an egg beater. Next, hide the object behind a box or felt board. Make noise with each object and see if the children can guess what item you are using. Repeat using all the items. Ask the children to listen to the people in their family. Does someone sniffle, sigh, or shuffle their feet? Have them listen for someone singing, cooing, or tapping their fingers.

Art Activity: Make a Shape Pole

Many Indian tribes in the northwestern United States made totem poles to record their family history. Show the children pictures of totem poles. Precut familiar shapes like circles, squares, rectangles, and triangles from five-inch squares of colorful construction paper. Let the children make a "shape pole" by pasting various shapes vertically on a large piece of paper.

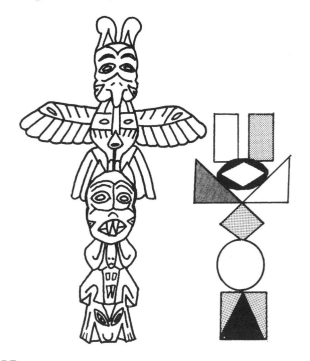

Language Activity: Talk about Families

Ask the children what activities their families like to do together. To get them started you may have to suggest some things like reading, eating, chores, gardening, raking leaves, and taking walks. You can also bring pictures from magazines to start the conversation. Be sure to let everyone talk.

Active Game: This is the Way

To the tune of "The Mulberry Bush" sing and act out the activities the children mentioned in the previous language activity. Use the following words for the first verse:

> This is the way we rake the leaves,
> Rake the leaves, rake the leaves,
> This is the way we rake the leaves,
> Early in the morning.

Then substitute the activities they enjoy doing with their families for the next verses.

Cassette source: *Playtime Parade* by Patti Dallas and Laura Baron. Yellow Springs, Ohio: Golden Glow, 1989.

Music source: *Jane Yolen's Mother Goose Songbook.* Honesdale, Pa.: Boyds Mill, 1992.

Resources for Story Time

Poems

"Two Little Sisters Went Walking One Day." From *Chinese Mother Goose Rhymes*, edited by Robert Wyndham. Cleveland: World Publishing, 1968.

Nice illustration by Ed Young with Chinese characters along with the English words.

"Fambly Time," by Eloise Greenfield. From *Night On Neighborhood Street.* New York: Dial, 1991.

A beautiful double-page illustration of an African American family.

Books

Baby-0 by Nancy White Carlstrom. Boston: Little Brown, 1992.

A West Indian family gets ready for market and sings a song about each family member.

So Much by Trish Cooke. Cambridge, Mass.: Candlewick, 1994.

Relatives arrive and cannot resist kissing and squeezing the baby.

My Cousin Katie by Michael Garland. New York: Crowell, 1989.

Katie's cousin tells what she loves about the farm including Katie.

Treasure Nap by Juanita Havill. Boston: Houghton, 1992.

A little girl hears the story of her Mexican family's immigration to America.

Do Like Kyla by Angela Johnson. New York: Orchard, 1990.

A young African American girl copies her older sister, Kyla.

Two Greedy Bears by Mirra Ginsburg. New York: Macmillan, 1976.

A sly fox tricks two bear cubs who insist on equal shares. A Hungarian tale.

Jamaica Tag-Along by Juanita Havill. Boston: Houghton Mifflin, 1989.

Big brother will not let Jamaica tag along with him, but she welcomes a younger child who wants to play with her.

Tucking Mommy In by Morag Loh. New York: Orchard, 1987.

Two little girls put their exhausted Mommy to bed.

Guess How Much I Love You by Sam McBratney. Cambridge, Mass.: Candlewick, 1995.

Little Nutbrown Hare and his father play a game by topping each other's expression of love in this charming bedtime story.

Anansi the Spider by Gerald McDermott. New York: Holt, 1972.

Each of his six sons use their special talents to save Anansi. African folktale.

The Keeping Quilt by Patricia Polacco. New York: Simon and Schuster, 1988.

A quilt is passed through four generations of an immigrant Jewish family.

Mother, Mother, I Want Another by Maria Polushkin. New York: Crown, 1978.

A fanciful story of a mouse whose mother misunderstands and gives him other mothers instead of another kiss.

Dumpling Soup by Jama Kim Rattigan. Boston: Little Brown, 1993.

In this longer story, Marisa, a young Hawaiian girl, makes dumplings for the New Year's festivities of her big family.

Con Mi Hermano, With My Brother by Eileen Roe. New York: Bradbury, 1991.

A boy wants to be like his older brother. The text is in English and Spanish.

The Relatives Came by Cynthia Rylant. New York: Bradbury, 1985.

A celebration of a visit from Virginia kin.

On Mother's Lap by Ann Scott. New York: Clarion, 1992.

An Eskimo mother reassures her son that there is always room for him on his mother's lap, even with a new baby.

Homeplace by Anne Shelby. New York: Orchard, 1995.

A grandmother and her grandchild trace their family's history in their rambling farm house.

Through Moon and Stars and Night Skies by Ann Turner. New York: Harper & Row, 1990.

A boy tells the events from the time he left his native land, a place far away, to when he arrived in his new home with his adoptive parents.

Music

"Free to Be…A Family." Cassette source: *Free To Be A Family* by Marlo Thomas & Friends. Hollywood, Calif.: A & M Records, 1988.

In this cassette entirely about families, the first song celebrates family differences.

"Something for Everyone." Cassette source: *Free To Be A Family* by Marlo Thomas & Friends. Hollywood, Calif.: A & M Records, 1988.

A lively song about family possibilities. It lists people who might be part of a family and places a family might live including a castle or a riverboat. Third song on the tape.

Video

"Mom and Me." From *We All Sing Together*. New York: Children's Television Workshop, 1993.

A short song-video about family diversity. Located about halfway into the tape.